The New Moon Race

Soyuz spacecraft launch   NASA

The New Moon Race

Morris Jones

ROSENBERG

First published in Australia in 2009
by Rosenberg Publishing Pty Ltd
PO Box 6125, Dural Delivery Centre NSW 2158
Phone: +61 2 9654 1502 Fax: 61 2 9654 1338
Email: rosenbergpub@smartchat.net.au
Web: www.rosenbergpub.com.au

National Library of Australia Cataloguing-in-Publication data:
Jones, Morris, 1971-
The new moon race / Morris Jones.
1st ed.
ISBN 9781877058820 (hbk.)
Includes index.
Bibliography.
Moon—Exploration.
Lunar bases.
Space race.
Astronautics--Forecasting.

629.454

Set in 14 on 16 point Verlag Book
Printed in China by Everbest Printing Co Limited

10 9 8 7 6 5 4 3 2 1

Contents

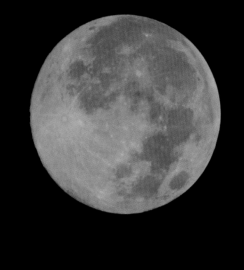

Moon, seen from the International Space Station   NASA

Introduction

In 1969, Neil Armstrong and Buzz Aldrin became the first humans to set foot on another world.

Sending astronauts to the Moon was the climax of a frantic, exciting period of spaceflight. The space age had begun in 1957, when the Soviet Union launched Sputnik, the world's first artificial satellite. The world had been amazed by this achievement, and also shocked. Satellites and the rockets that launched them had the potential to upset a very fragile balance of power between the United States of America and the Union of Soviet Socialist Republics. America's supremacy was challenged by a hostile superpower, armed with nuclear weapons and huge military forces. On Earth, as in space, a desperate struggle for power and survival was unfolding.

The fears and passions unleashed by this volatile scenario propelled the United States to invest heavily in space exploration. Desperate to match Soviet achievements in space, America developed the Apollo program, designed to send astronauts to the Moon before the end of the 1960s. A frantic pace of missions ensued, culminating in the mission of Apollo 11 in July 1969. The flag of the United States of America was triumphantly planted in the grey lunar soil, together with the footprints of her astronauts. The Soviet Union had been beaten to this major goal in the 'space race'.

Five more Apollo missions would take astronauts to the surface of the Moon. Apollo 17 returned to Earth in 1972, wrapping up the most amazing phase of human spaceflight ever undertaken.

But greater feats were expected. The Apollo program was thought to be the opening act in a long series of grand achievements in space. Before the turn of the century, it was expected that astronauts would return to the Moon, build bases there, and

head onwards to Mars.

It didn't happen. Politics, economics, technology and other factors kept humans away from the Moon. The 'space race' settled down into a relaxed pace, devoid of the shocks of the 1960s.

There will be no humans on the Moon on the 40th anniversary of the landing of Apollo 11. Nobody has set foot there in more than 36 years.

But the world is returning to the Moon. Robot missions are exploring its surface, and preparing for humans to follow. The stage is set for a new chapter in space exploration. New discoveries await us. New adventures will unfold. The years ahead will be among the most interesting ever witnessed in the history of spaceflight.

Earthrise above the Moon's horizon, seen from Apollo 11   NASA

1 About the Moon

We are lucky to have the Moon as our nearest neighbour in space. It's quite unusual for a small planet such as Earth to have such a large companion in orbit. We also depend on the Moon for our lives. The orbit of the Moon stabilises the rotational axis of the Earth, preventing it from shifting wildly. Without the Moon, weather patterns and climate on Earth would be extremely hostile. The Moon also governs our tides and bathes our night skies in reflected light.

The Moon's diameter is 3,476 kilometres, roughly a quarter of the Earth's 12,756 kilometres. See the two

worlds from space, and you are treated to two vastly different sights. The blue Earth, girded by gentle swirls of water vapour clouds, speaks of life. The Moon, by contrast, is barren grey. It has no liquid water, no atmosphere, and almost certainly no life.

But the Earth and Moon are more closely related than just by proximity. They are made of similar rocky material. Scientists think that the Moon was formed billions of years ago, as the Solar System was still chaotic and forming. A small planet, probably half the size of Earth today, collided with our home planet. Debris from this massive event was thrown into space, and some of it aggregated to form the Moon. Thus, the Moon is a product of the early Earth and a world that no longer exists.

The Moon takes roughly 28 days to orbit the Earth, and is roughly 384,400 kilometres away. Gravity on the surface is roughly one-sixth that of Earth.

The Moon's surface is dominated by light patches of grey rock, which have been eroded and baked by direct exposure to outer space. Dark patches of rock, known as 'seas', are the solidified remains of basaltic lava flows.

The Moon's temperature during the day rises to more than 100° Celsius. It's almost –200° Celsius at night. The lack of an atmosphere, and the two-week length of each night and day,

Far side of the Moon, from the Galileo spacecraft   NASA/JPL

contribute to these extremes.

The Moon constantly points one face to Earth, making it impossible to see the 'far side' directly from Earth. Curiously, the far side is more heavily cratered, and contains fewer basaltic lava seas, than the near side.

Near side of the Moon, from Apollo 11   NASA

2 A Brief History of Lunar Exploration

Look Up!

The Moon was the first world beyond Earth to be studied extensively. It's so close that almost anyone can see it. Humans have been exploring the Moon since prehistoric times. You can see the phases of the Moon change over 28 days, and observe its dark and light patches.

The invention of the telescope gave scientists a closer look. Craters became visible, along with mountains and valleys. But roughly half the Moon's surface had never been seen. The 'far side' of the Moon never faces Earth. Nobody knew what lay just beyond their direct line of sight.

Like the sailors of ancient times who created tales of sea monsters, amazing stories were generated about the state of the Moon. But these were not wild legends spun by storytellers. They were valid scientific theories invented by professional scientists. With no way to reach the Moon, or even examine it closely, nobody really knew what was there. Some scientists worried that the Moon was covered with a deep sea of fine dust. Astronauts who landed there would sink rapidly and disappear.

The advent of spaceflight offered ways to find out. For millennia, people could do no more than simply gaze up at this other world, and wonder what

was there. So much could be seen, yet so many questions remained. The temptation to finally reach something that had been beyond our grasp for so long was irresistible.

Hit the Moon

Unsurprisingly, attempts to reach the Moon began shortly after the launch of the first satellite. The first lunar probes were simple devices, usually designed to simply hit the Moon, or fly past it. Like the first Earth satellites, these lunar probes were small capsules filled with some simple instruments. They could measure the radiation and electrical fields around them, and do little else.

No humans had been launched into space by the end of the 1950s. But the 'space race' had already targeted the Moon as a goal. This early focus on the Moon, so soon after the October 1957 launch of Sputnik, helped to set the stage for more ambitious plans in the 1960s.

The Soviet Union made a handful of quiet attempts to launch small capsules to the Moon in 1958, but all of them experienced problems with their rockets during the launch phase. The United States made its first attempt to reach the Moon in August 1958. Like its Soviet rivals, its rocket malfunctioned. A second US launch attempt sent a spacecraft dubbed Pioneer 1 almost a third of the way to the Moon in October 1958. But its rocket did not provide enough thrust for Pioneer 1 to reach its target, and it fell back to Earth. If Pioneer 1 had reached its goal, an attempt would have been made to place it in orbit around the Moon, by firing a retro-rocket.

Pioneer 3, a tiny probe with an even simpler design than Pioneer 1, made a similar journey to roughly a third of the Earth–Moon distance in December 1958. This had been an attempt to simply fly past the Moon.

The Soviet Union launched a probe dubbed Luna 1 in January 1959. This

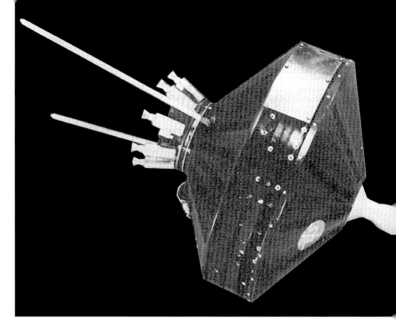

Pioneer 1   NASA

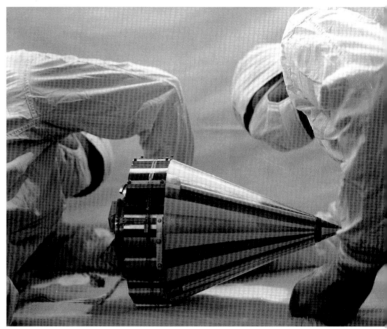

Pioneer 3   NASA

was apparently an attempt to hit the surface of the Moon. Luna 1 missed its target, but it managed to fly past the Moon and enter orbit around the Sun, the first artificial space probe to do so. The United States matched the feat in March 1959, when Pioneer 4 (identical in design to Pioneer 3) became the first American spacecraft to fly past the Moon.

The Soviets reached another step in September 1959, when Luna 2 became the first object launched from Earth to

Pioneer 1 launch   NASA

reach the surface of the Moon. The probe was destroyed on impact (it had not been designed to land softly), but medals struck with the coat of arms of the Soviet Union had been deposited on the lunar surface.

Less than a month later, on the second anniversary of the launch of Sputnik, the Soviet Union launched Luna 3. This was the most sophisticated and successful lunar mission to date. Luna 3 flew over the far side of the Moon and then travelled into orbit around the Sun. As it passed over the far side, a camera system took photographs of the lunar surface, developed them, and scanned the film for transmission to Earth. The photography was extremely crude, but it was the first attempt to view the far side of the Moon.

The Challenge of Apollo
In 1961, the Soviet Union launched the first man into space. Yuri Gagarin made one orbit of the Earth and returned safely. The flight was another blow to American pride, and added to the perceived geopolitical strength of the Soviet Union. Soon afterwards, Alan Shepard was launched by the United States on a sub-orbital mission into space. Sending humans into space escalated the profile and the sophistication of this rivalry for space achievements.

US President John F. Kennedy soon decided on a course of action that would dominate spaceflight for the years ahead. He proposed sending US astronauts to the Moon before the end of the decade. Generous funding

and technical support was provided by the US government for the Apollo program, which was soon developing the technology and the spacecraft that would be needed to reach the Moon.

Quietly, the Soviet Union was also drawing plans to send its own cosmonauts to the Moon.

More Robots
The creation of the Apollo program provided a renewed intensity to the idea of exploring the Moon with robotic space probes. The earliest probes had been motivated by scientific curiosity, national prestige and a sense of adventure. Now, there was also a need to ensure that the Moon would be safe for human explorers.

The next sequence of US lunar probes was dubbed Ranger, and involved larger and more sophisticated spacecraft with solar panels to provide power. Ranger was designed to photograph the Moon closely as it flew towards the surface. It was even hoped that a simple capsule, with a seismometer, could be landed safely. But the earliest Ranger probes were failures. The first two missions, launched in 1961, didn't leave Earth orbit. Ranger 3 made it further into space, but still failed to reach the Moon. In 1962, Ranger 4 crashed into the Moon without landing its capsule, and Ranger 5 missed the Moon entirely. Afterwards, the spacecraft's design was changed to carry nothing more than cameras, which would observe the moon closely as the spacecraft plunged to destruction on the surface. But Ranger 6, launched

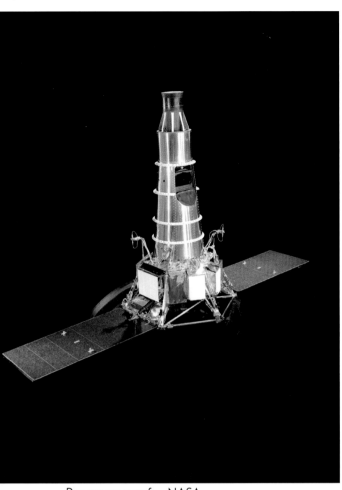

Ranger spacecraft   NASA

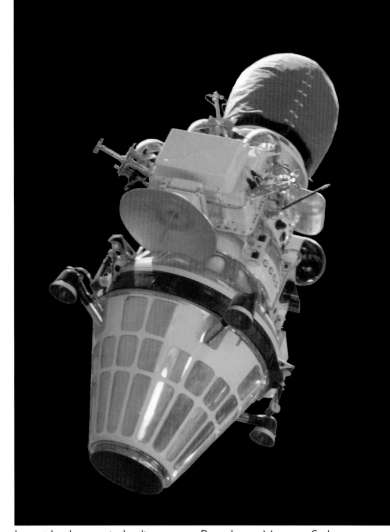

Luna 9 lander atop its landing stage   Powerhouse Museum, Sydney

in early 1964, experienced a failure of its cameras. Finally, Ranger 7, launched in July 1964, became the first of its series to complete a successful mission. Features on the lunar surface gradually grew larger and sharper in the pictures returned to Earth as the spacecraft drew closer to the surface. Transmissions abruptly stopped on impact. Ranger 8 and Ranger 9, both launched in 1965, also flew successful missions.

While American astronauts and Soviet cosmonauts orbited the Earth, the Soviet Union continued its own robotic exploration of the Moon. After another string of failures, Luna 9 became the first spacecraft to safely touch down on the moon in January 1966. The lander was an egg-shaped capsule that rode to the Moon on top of a rocket stage. The rocket fired to brake the lander's speed as it approached the Moon. Then the lander was separated. It inflated airbags to cushion its impact. After it had stopped moving, four petal-like panels opened on the 'egg' to push the lander upright and expose its instruments. A similar landing technique would be used decades later, in 1997, when the US Mars Pathfinder mission also used airbags and a petal enclosure to land on Mars. Luna 9 provided the first close-up views of the surface of the Moon. Later that year, Luna 13, a spacecraft with a similar design, would also land on the Moon.

The United States would also achieve its first touchdown on the Moon in 1966, when Surveyor 1 landed safely. The Surveyor probes had three footpads, and tested some of the procedures that in the future would be used to land Apollo astronauts on the Moon. Later Surveyor landers also carried a robot arm that could be used to scoop lunar soil, and instruments to check the mineral content of the lunar soil.

The first spacecraft to be placed in orbit around the Moon was also a Soviet probe. Luna 10 was launched in 1966. It was not designed to take pictures. Later that year, Luna 11 entered orbit and beamed back better images than Luna 3 had produced. But the most sophisticated orbiters

launched during this phase of lunar exploration were American. Five Lunar Orbiter spacecraft were sent to produce detailed photographs of the lunar surface from orbit. The goal was to map almost the entire surface of the Moon to help select landing sites for the Apollo missions. Flying between 1966 and 1967, the lunar orbiters produced detailed pictures that sometimes revealed features as small as two metres across. This photographic resolution is considered good by twenty-first century standards, but it was all done with 1960s-era film cameras and simple scanners on board the spacecraft! Another US lunar orbiting spacecraft, Explorer 35, was launched in 1967 to study fields and particles in the space around the Moon.

Lunar Orbiter   NASA

THE NEW MOON RACE

Surveyor 1 photographs its own shadow   NASA

The Race Quickens

By 1967, the Apollo program was approaching its maturity, but tensions were rising. The year had opened with tragedy. In January, the three members of the crew of Apollo 1 were killed in a fire inside the spacecraft during an engineering test. This prompted a re-design of many components of the spacecraft. Weeks later, the Soviet Union would launch its first Soyuz spacecraft, a manned capsule that rivalled the capabilities of Apollo. But its sole occupant would die when his malfunctioning spacecraft crashed during the return to Earth.

Following a series of unmanned test launches, the United States launched Apollo 7 as the first Apollo mission with a crew on board in 1968. It merely orbited the Earth. Apollo 8, launched in December 1968, would fly all the way to the Moon and enter orbit. The crew broadcast live pictures of the Moon on Christmas Eve to thrilled television viewers around the world. The mission

did not carry a lunar module, and no attempt was made to land on the Moon.

The Soviet Union had also been developing plans to send cosmonauts to the Moon. A series of spacecraft dubbed 'Zond' had been flown to the Moon and back to Earth. These had not carried any humans, but at least one Zond mission carried animals. The first Zond spacecraft to reach the Moon was launched in September 1968. A second launch occurred a month later. These missions, flown just before the flight of Apollo 8, raised concerns that Soviet cosmonauts would reach the Moon before the Americans. The Zond missions were practice runs for sending Soviet cosmonauts on identical spacecraft.

Astronauts on the Moon

Further Apollo missions in 1969 would test the lunar module in Earth orbit, then test it in orbit around the Moon. Finally, in July 1969, Apollo 11 was launched to land the first astronauts on the Moon. The flight of Neil Armstrong, Buzz Aldrin and Michael Collins ranks among the most significant events of the twentieth century. On July 20, 1969 (US time), Armstrong and Aldrin landed on the surface, and later spent roughly two and a half hours walking on the Moon. They returned safely to Earth.

The success of Apollo 11 amazed the entire world. It boosted American prestige and dampened fears of Soviet superiority in space. Within the Soviet Union, news of the successful landing was downplayed. The Soviets would

15 orbited overhead. This was a new type of robot lander, designed to retrieve soil samples and return them to Earth. It was hoped that Luna 15 could return a capsule with moon dust before Apollo 11 returned to Earth. But it crashed as it attempted to land on the Moon.

After *Apollo 11*

Six more Apollo missions were launched to the Moon after Apollo 11. The near-tragedy of Apollo 13 is another legendary tale of spaceflight. Halfway to the Moon, an explosion on board the spacecraft destroyed most of the mission's power and life-support capabilities. The astronauts were forced to use supplies in the lunar module to stay alive while they navigated their crippled spacecraft back to Earth. Apollo 15 marked the first use of a lunar rover, a lightweight vehicle that allowed astronauts to drive on the Moon. Apollo 17 closed off the first phase of human exploration of the Moon in 1972.

The Quiet Moon

The Apollo missions had been so scientifically productive, and so expensive, that interest in lunar exploration waned in the United States during the rest of the 1970s. Attention was focused on sending robot probes to other planets, and developing the space shuttle to launch astronauts into Earth orbit. The United States and the Soviet Union also developed space stations that allowed humans to live in space for lengthy intervals.

Digesting the results of the Apollo

Buzz Aldrin, Apollo 11, walks on the Moon   NASA

officially deny the existence of their own plans to send cosmonauts to the Moon for decades, despite evidence to the contrary. Plans for sending astronauts to the surface, or even sending them to fly around the Moon on a Zond spacecraft, were quietly shelved in the years to follow.

But the Soviets had made one last-ditch effort to upstage the achievements of Apollo 11. As the astronauts prepared to explore the Moon, a robot probe dubbed Luna

THE NEW MOON RACE

missions would take decades. Moon rocks were examined at sites around the world. Instruments left on the moon by the Apollo astronauts continued to function.

The United States placed a radio astronomy satellite (Explorer 49) in orbit around the Moon in 1973. But this was not really an attempt to explore the Moon. It was used as a convenient orbital anchor point away from the Earth. The Moon also served as a natural shield from radio interference from Earth at some points in the satellite's orbit.

The Soviet Union continued to send robot missions to the Moon. In 1970, Luna 16 landed and retrieved soil samples. These were returned to the Soviet Union inside a tiny spherical capsule. Later that year, a large robot lunar rover called Lunokhod 1 touched down. This drove across the surface by remote control, returning television pictures.

A second sample return mission, Luna 20, would touch down in 1972. Lunokhod 2, a second lunar rover, arrived in 1973. The final Soviet lunar mission for the decade was Luna 24, the third and final mission to return rock and soil samples. It landed in August 1976.

Afterwards, efforts to explore the Moon with spacecraft would enter a long period of inactivity.

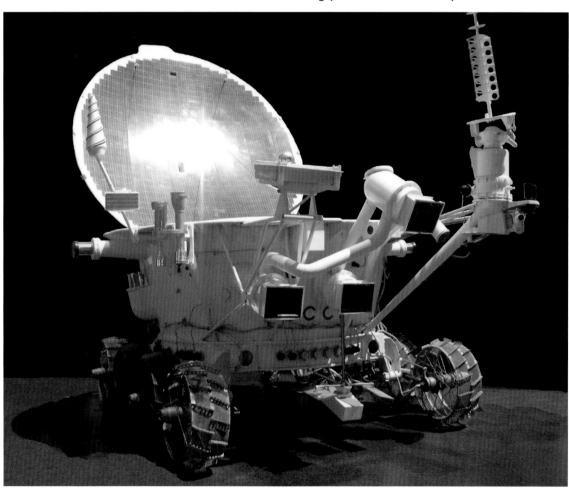

Lunokhod rover   Powerhouse Museum, Sydney

3 The Gap Years

The end of the 1970s and the 1980s represented a long sequence of 'gap years' in lunar exploration. No spacecraft were launched to explore the Moon during this timeframe. But this didn't stop people from thinking about the next steps in exploring the Moon. Apollo had provided wonderful samples and data, but more remained to be discovered.

A False Start

In 1989, on the twentieth anniversary of the landing of Apollo 11, US President George H.W. Bush attempted to kick-start a return to the Moon. He announced plans for a broad strategy of missions that came to be known as the Space Exploration Initiative. Under the plan, American astronauts would return to the Moon, build bases there, and eventually travel onwards to Mars. But the project would have required massive funding, and lacked political appeal. It failed to attract support from lawmakers, and quickly disappeared.

Funding for spaceflight in the United States has never approached the massive levels expended in the 1960s at any other time since.

The Moral of Apollo

The failure of the Space Exploration Initiative highlighted the unique conditions that gave rise to the Apollo program. In the early 1960s, space exploration was new. It captured the attention and imagination of the public and aroused serious concerns over national security. Some analysts were concerned that a nation that dominated space could also dominate the Earth. Reaching the Moon was almost like seizing land on Earth. It was strongly felt that America had to go there first to defend its interests and its position as the world's most powerful nation.

America was also wrestling with regional conflicts around the world, such as the Vietnam War, and a failed attempt to depose a Soviet-backed government in Cuba. In all these cases, America was essentially struggling against Soviet proxy armies and governments. Adding a race to the Moon seemed like a natural extension of superpower rivalry.

So the Apollo program was largely propelled by politics, international relations and national security issues.

By 1989, the world had changed dramatically. The Soviet Union was weakening, and the United States no longer felt as threatened as it did when the Cold War was at its height. Space exploration had also lost much of its novelty for the general public.

Spaceflight historians are generally amazed at the way that the Apollo program was able to generate so much support, so quickly. They have also warned that the unusual mix of conditions that allowed it to be created in 1961 is unlikely to be repeated in the near future. Attempts to garner substantial support for massive lunar missions will require different combinations of funding and justification. A failure to understand the complex influence of politics, economics, international relations and public support has been the downfall of many 'false starts' in spaceflight.

The New Foundations

Nevertheless, exploration of the Moon has been renewed in recent years. The motivations are different, and arguably more complex, than during the Apollo years. The result is a different mix of missions and nations participating in this new wave of spaceflight.

Far side of the Moon   NASA

A number of nations are taking their first steps towards the Moon for reasons similar to the Apollo program. Sending a probe to the Moon is a logical target for nations with strong economies. There are domestic political benefits, along with demonstrations of strength to the rest of the world. Scientific returns are also enough to justify some low-cost missions. Public interest is still strong for unlocking some of the Moon's greatest mysteries. Some groups also see the Moon as a commercial frontier, or a source of minerals and energy. The spectre of future lunar territorial claims has faded, but it has not disappeared.

So the next chapter of spaceflight to the Moon is likely to generate a satisfying course of surprises and adventure. It's also worth remembering that, despite the dozens of missions that have been sent there, the Moon remains largely unexplored.

Viking lander on Mars   NASA

4 Life After Apollo

Decades after Armstrong and Aldrin placed the first human footprints on the Moon, the only humans to have landed there since are ten other Apollo moonwalkers. At NASA, the Moon was abandoned as a goal for human spaceflight after the Apollo program. Apollo had been a hugely expensive undertaking, and budgets were being trimmed even as astronauts were walking on the surface. NASA had originally planned to send Apollo 18, Apollo 19 and Apollo 20 to land astronauts on the Moon. But there would be no more landings after Apollo 17.

Exploring the Planets

As the 1970s unfolded, a new theme emerged in spaceflight. Exploring the planets with robot probes attracted the attention of space agencies, scientists and the general public. The Moon seemed to have been fairly well explored in the first phase of the space age, and it was time to look further outwards. In this decade, missions were launched by the United States and the Soviet Union to every planet in the solar system. (In fact, the small outer world of Pluto was not targeted, but its status as a planet has since been called into question.) Mercury was photographed from a distance by the NASA Mariner 10 probe, and the Soviet Union managed to land a probe on the surface of Venus. But two missions stand out as the premier achievements of 1970s' planetary exploration.

The Viking missions to Mars were launched by NASA in 1975, and arrived in 1976. Two identical spacecraft were launched, each consisting of an orbiter and a large lander. The Viking missions became the first spacecraft to return scientific data from the surface of Mars, producing stunning vistas of ochre plains beneath pink Martian skies. The landers also tested the soil for life. The biological experiments produced some strange chemical reactions in the soil, but these are generally not regarded as the product of living creatures. Nevertheless, controversy over the results has persisted for decades.

The twin Voyager spacecraft were launched in 1977, and were aimed at the outer planets. The spacecraft would fly past their targets rapidly, snapping pictures as they approached and departed. Voyager 1 and Voyager 2 flew past Jupiter, returning the first detailed images of this world. They then headed out to Saturn. Here, Voyager 1 was targeted on a trajectory that took it out of the orbital planes of the planets. Voyager 2 flew onwards to Uranus in 1986 and Neptune in 1989. Over 30 years after their launch, both craft are still operational, and are detecting evidence of the interaction between the Sun's particles and fields with interstellar space at the 'edge' of

Voyager spacecraft   NASA

Jupiter, as seen by Voyager   NASA

the solar system.

The scientific data and photography from this wave of planetary exploration was captivating. But US planetary exploration entered a long period of dormancy in the 1980s. Despite the ongoing missions of the Voyagers, no new planetary missions were launched in most of this decade. Finally, in 1989, the spacecraft Galileo was launched to orbit Jupiter. Its main dish antenna, designed to unfurl in space like an umbrella, did not deploy. But the

Voyager view of Saturn   NASA

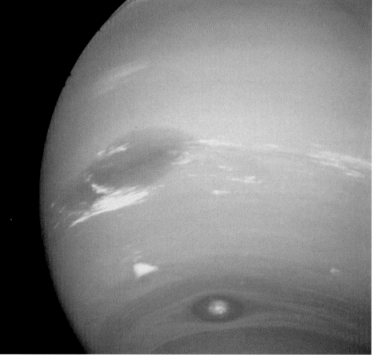

Neptune, last planet visited by Voyager 2   NASA

(Below) Cassini spacecraft at Saturn   NASA

mission still returned amazing pictures and data through back-up antennas.

In 1997, the spacecraft Cassini was launched to orbit Saturn. Also in 1997, the small spacecraft Mars Pathfinder landed on Mars with the aid of a unique airbag landing system. It was the first probe to land there since the Viking missions. Mars has been an ongoing target of planetary exploration ever since. The most prominent missions so far have been the Mars Exploration Rovers, which landed in 2004 and have remained functional for years.

Pluto was targeted by the launch of the spacecraft New Horizons by the United States in 2006. It will arrive at Pluto in 2015.

The success of this planetary exploration carried the hopes of spaceflight enthusiasts through a relatively dry period of human spaceflight for the United States caused by the demise of the Apollo program.

The Space Shuttle

In the early 1970s, NASA refocused on a new goal for human spaceflight: sending astronauts into orbit on a regular basis. A new type of vehicle, dubbed the Space Shuttle, was proposed. The Space Shuttle was like a winged aircraft that would fly into space like a rocket, and land like a glider. Unlike the Saturn 5 rockets and Apollo spacecraft that had flown to the Moon, the Space Shuttle would be re-useable. It would carry a larger crew and sport an enormous cargo bay for carrying equipment into space and back. The Space Shuttle would permit the construction of a large space station in Earth orbit, and fly more cheaply than any previous spaceship.

Or so NASA hoped. While the Space Shuttle was in development, NASA used a leftover Saturn 5 rocket (originally designated for a Moon mission) to launch Skylab, an experimental space station built around the converted third stage of this rocket. Three crews of astronauts were launched to Skylab on board Apollo spacecraft. In 1975, the last Apollo spacecraft carried three astronauts to a rendezvous with a Soyuz spacecraft launched by the Soviet Union. The two spacecraft were able to dock with Skylab by means of a special adaptor that carried docking ports for both. Afterwards, US astronauts would remain grounded for years while they waited for the Space Shuttle to reach the launch pad. Delays to the introduction of this complex vehicle mounted.

The Soviet Union made steady progress with its own spaceflight ambitions during the 1970s and 1980s. Talk of sending cosmonauts to the Moon was taboo, and the Soviet Union still officially denied that such plans had ever existed. The Soviets developed a sequence of Salyut space stations, launching their first in 1971. Crews would be launched to the stations on board Soyuz capsule spacecraft, which would dock with the stations, and wait inactively like a parked car until the end of a mission. Sadly, the first Salyut crew died on their return to Earth when the atmosphere leaked out of their Soyuz

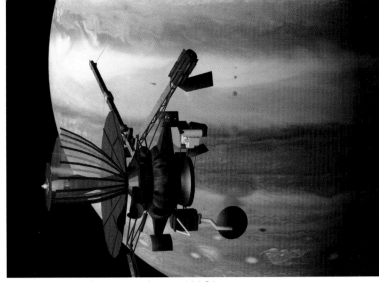

Galileo spacecraft arrives at Jupiter NASA

Mars Exploration Rover   NASA

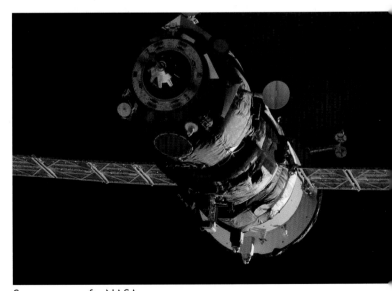

Soyuz spacecraft NASA

capsule. In 1982, the Salyut 7 space station was launched, marking the end of the Salyut stations. Salyut 6 and Salyut 7 also received new supplies on a regular basis from unmanned Progress cargo spacecraft, which were like modified Soyuz spacecraft.

Soviet expertise in space stations reached its pinnacle in 1986, when the Mir Space Station was launched. This was gradually expanded with the addition of new modules launched by separate rockets.

The Space Shuttle made its first launch in 1981. Amazing feats were achieved as astronauts flew out from the shuttle with jet backpacks to rescue stranded satellites, and the Hubble Space Telescope was placed in orbit. But overall, the Space Shuttle turned out to be an expensive and cumbersome vehicle to operate. The loss of the shuttle Challenger in a launch explosion in 1986, and the

Russian cosmonaut aboard the Mir Space Station   NASA

THE NEW MOON RACE

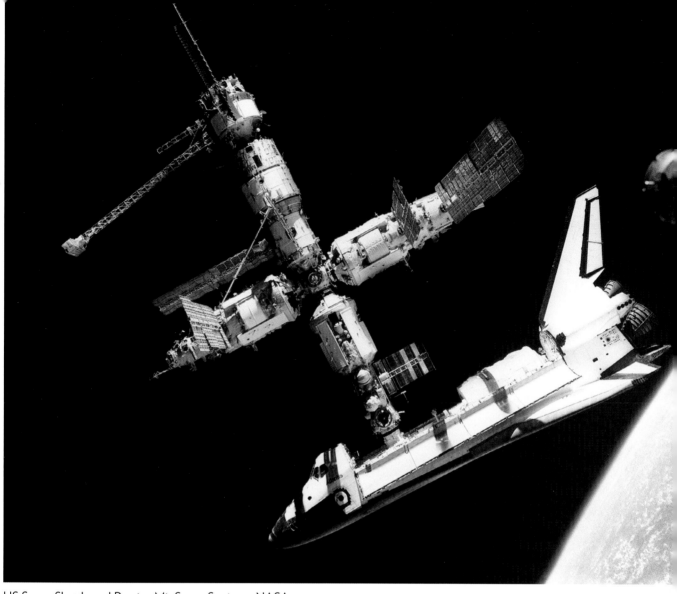

US Space Shuttle and Russian Mir Space Station   NASA

destruction of the shuttle Columbia during re-entry in 2003, highlighted its design flaws.

The Soyuz spacecraft remained the only Soviet vehicle capable of carrying humans into orbit. The Soviet Union embarked on an abortive project to develop their own space shuttle, but shelved the plan due to its overwhelming costs. The Buran Shuttle made only a single unmanned test flight before it was mothballed. Soyuz seemed like a poor rival to the US Space Shuttle for many years. It was a small capsule spacecraft, less roomy and impressive than the mighty winged

Space Shuttle photographed from the International Space Station   NASA

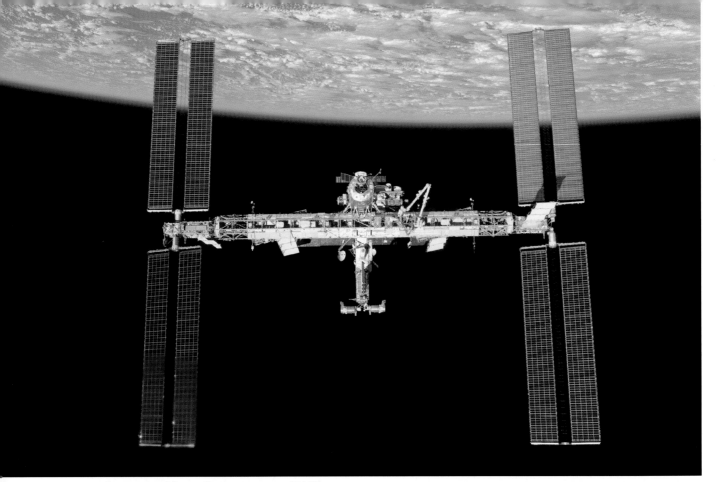

International Space Station in 2007   NASA

vehicle flown by America. But Soyuz has steadily earned a reputation as the most reliable human space launch system ever developed.

Following on from the first flights of the shuttle, NASA drew plans for a new space station. The 1980s and 1990s saw a frustrating saga of cost cuts and redesigns of the original space station project, which included participation from the European Space Agency, Japan, Canada and other nations. Delays set in. Following the collapse of the Soviet Union, Russia was incorporated as a partner in the newly named International Space Station. As a prelude to the construction of the new station, NASA conducted practice docking runs and crew transfers with the Russian Mir space station.

The first module for this new space station was launched by a Russian Proton rocket in 1998. A module was soon attached by a US space shuttle. Then the pace of construction slackened as delays with its launch vehicles and parts set in. Already behind schedule by roughly a decade, the space station was becoming another failing spaceflight project. Crews were delivered to the station and work was performed, but the general public seemed uninterested.

The early years of the twenty-first century saw NASA struggling to manage its space shuttle and space station programs. The loss of Columbia in 2003 seriously delayed both. Soon, it seemed that the United States was looking for exit strategies from both programs.

It was decided to restrict the future

Russian Progress cargo ship, based on the design of Soyuz   NASA

number of Shuttle launches, and aim to retire the vehicle around the year 2010. NASA's participation in the International Space Station would extend for a few years beyond this, but probably not much further. Recent events suggest that the Shuttle could fly for a few years beyond this original retirement date, but it will not be operational for much longer.

Something else needed to be done to give America a long-term future in spaceflight. NASA was in need of a mission, and a credible means of achieving it. For decades, space activists had been urging the US government to send astronauts to Mars. But such a mission would exceed the budgets and the technical prowess that NASA could expect to muster in the near future.

Operations in Earth orbit had proven to be uninspiring. So the best option for NASA's new direction seemed to be a return to the Moon. It would not be possible to duplicate the frantic pace of missions, or the copious levels of funding, that NASA experienced in the 1960s. But a carefully managed program could send astronauts back to the Moon, and achieve far more than Apollo.

NASA could cite years of spaceflight experience and better technology as head-starts for its return to the Moon, and by 2004 plans to return American astronauts to the Moon were solidifying.

Will the planned return happen as NASA expects? Nobody knows for sure. Recent events in NASA's history have bolstered the calls of sceptics. But an overall trend of America, and the rest of the world, returning to the Moon

5 The Second Wave

Plans for a grand return to the Moon faltered in the 1980s, and for more than a decade no spacecraft went there. But the 1990s saw a return to the Moon through somewhat backhanded channels, as opportunities arose. Each mission had its own unique combination of goals and driving forces, some of them never seen before in lunar spacecraft.

Hiten

The 1970s and 1980s saw the emergence of space programs in countries beyond the United States and the Soviet Union. China, India, Europe and Japan were now so advanced that they could launch their own satellites on their own rockets. The launch of the first Japanese mission to the Moon in

1990 heralded this growing diversity in spaceflight.

Hiten (named for a Buddhist angel) was a modest first step for Japan's lunar program. In fact, the spacecraft wasn't really designed to explore the Moon at all. It was a stubby cylinder just 1.4 metres in diameter, and carried no cameras or instruments for probing the lunar surface. Hiten's main goal was simply to fly through space, testing the components on board the spacecraft, and also demonstrating some unique fuel-saving manoeuvres. The only scientific instrument was a dust counter that measured collisions with tiny particles in space.

Hiten was placed into orbit around the Earth, and soon began a carefully timed dance with the Moon's gravity. Most lunar probes use powerful rocket motors to send them towards the Moon, but Hiten steadily stretched its orbit deeper into space, using the Moon's gravity to nudge it steadily away from the Earth. The effect was small, but over a long period of time, Hiten simply drew closer to the Moon. Eventually, the probe drew so close that it was able to fire a tiny sub-satellite, just larger than a basketball, into orbit around the Moon. The sub-satellite's transmitter failed, but Japan had at least lobbed an object into lunar orbit.

Eventually, Hiten itself was placed in orbit around the Moon, after

Hiten spacecraft   JAXA

performing some more gravity dances on its trajectory. The spacecraft was deliberately crashed into the Moon in 1993.

The flight of Hiten had fulfilled its goals of testing satellite components and navigational techniques. But it also showed that lunar missions could be flown through indirect means—a spacecraft had reached the Moon when exploring the Moon wasn't really its main goal.

Galileo

Galileo was a massive and complex mission to Jupiter launched by NASA, America's space agency. The spacecraft was nudged out of the payload bay of a space shuttle in 1989, and then fired its rocket motor to begin a long journey to its goal.

Galileo's booster rocket wasn't powerful enough to send it directly to Jupiter. But it could pick up extra speed using a technique called 'gravity assist'. Like a skateboarder riding down a ramp, spacecraft are targeted at large objects (planets) and allowed to fall into their gravitational fields. They speed up, and also change their direction of travel. By carefully timing the approach, the spacecraft rides out of the gravitational field at a faster rate than it entered. Galileo had to make one gravity-assist run at the planet Venus, and two at Earth (in 1990 and 1992), to pick up enough speed to reach Jupiter.

Galileo took some nice pictures of Earth as it approached its planet of origin. But it also managed to

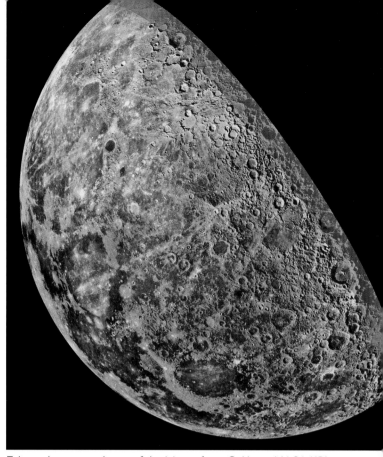

False-colour mineral map of the Moon, from Galileo   NASA/JPL

(Below) Athena 2 rocket prepares to launch Lunar Prospector NASA/KSC

photograph the Moon as it passed by. The Moon had been mapped and repeatedly photographed by spacecraft for decades, but Galileo still managed to produce surprises. The spacecraft's instruments were extremely advanced, able to spot specific types of minerals on the Moon by recording the way they reflected different bands of light. This technique is known as spectroscopy, and it's a common tool for examining objects in space.

Galileo also revealed some interesting details on a region known as the South Pole-Aitken Basin, which has not been well explored.

Again, Galileo wasn't really a Moon probe. It had visited Earth simply to pick up a free ride from its gravity. But photographing the Moon also allowed the spacecraft to test its cameras and instruments.

Clementine

Clementine was a small probe loaded with instruments that orbited the Moon and made amazing discoveries. But again, this was another backhanded approach to the Moon. Clementine was built by the US Department of Defense, and its main goal was

Clementine spacecraft in testing　Naval Research Laboratory

military. The spacecraft was designed to test sensors and miniaturised parts that could be used on future military satellites. Some of these were earmarked for ballistic missile defence systems.

But Clementine needed something to focus on during its flight. Sending the spacecraft to the Moon meant it had plenty to photograph.

Clementine was launched to the Moon in 1994, and was placed into a polar orbit. This took it over the north and south poles of the Moon, at right angles to the Moon's equator. The polar orbit is a traditional strategy for exploring other worlds. Gradually, as the moon or planet rotates, the polar orbit steadily moves the spacecraft across every point in the surface. This allows complete maps to be made.

Clementine produced the first overall map of the Moon since the lunar orbiters of the 1960s. With modern cameras, the photography was much better. Clementine also raised eyebrows with another experiment that

Clementine spacecraft in assembly　Naval Research Laboratory

it performed. A radar dish was used to beam pulses of radio waves at the polar regions of the Moon. The radar signal that bounced back was different from the signals from other parts of the Moon, and seemed to come from something very reflective. This strengthened the case for a theory that had excited the spaceflight community for years—there could be ice at the poles of the Moon.

Clementine's results didn't prove that ice existed at the poles, but they suggested it could be possible. Investigations would continue with other missions.

After two and a half months in lunar orbit, Clementine was sent on a new course, targeted at an asteroid called Geographos. Unfortunately, Clementine experienced a malfunction soon after leaving the Moon, and never reached its second goal. Yet few people were complaining. The mission had been a technical and a scientific triumph.

AsiaSat 3/HGS-1

In 1997, a commercial communications satellite dubbed AsiaSat 3 was left stranded in a low orbit by an underperforming rocket. It should have been sent into geostationary orbit, a ring around the Equator roughly 36,000 kilometres away. This is where most communications satellites lurk, for in this orbit they remain in a fixed position in the sky. Antennas can be pointed at the satellites without the need to constantly tilt them at a moving target.

Controllers wanted to nudge the satellite into the geostationary orbit belt using the satellite's on-board thrusters. Making a conventional ascent to this orbit would have required a lot of fuel, so the failed satellite launch was salvaged through the clever use of the Moon's gravity.

Thrusters on the satellite were used to send it on a trajectory to the Moon. Although this is much further out in space than geostationary orbit, it took less fuel to fly the satellite there than to reach geostationary orbit, then 'park' it in a specific orbital position. The Moon's gravity was used to bend the satellite's orbit, similar to the way that the Japanese Hiten spacecraft modified its own trajectory. The satellite, now renamed HGS-1 after an insurance payout on the failed launch, made two flybys of the Moon before it was successfully nestled into geostationary orbit. Although its fuel reserves had been greatly depleted, the satellite was still able to function for several years.

HGS-1 thus holds a place in history for the first practical use of crafty lunar-gravity flybys, which had previously only been used for demonstration purposes. The satellite carried no instruments for studying the Moon, and its owners had no initial plans for sending it there. But its rescue heralded the way for future uses of this navigation technique.

Lunar Prospector

At last, a mission focused on exploring the Moon, and nothing else! Lunar Prospector was a low-cost NASA mission aimed at mapping the mineral composition of the Moon and

Lunar Prospector spacecraft in launch preparation
NASA/KSC

searching for ice. The spacecraft was a stubby cylinder with instruments on booms. No conventional camera was carried. Lunar Prospector was launched to produce detailed chemical and rock studies that had not been performed by other missions, and to attempt to resolve the hotly debated question of water ice at the poles. It entered orbit around the moon in early 1998.

Lunar Prospector produced a detailed study of rock and soil compositions on the surface of the Moon, but the mission gained most of

its publicity from its work at the poles. An instrument known as a neutron spectrometer suggested that large amounts of hydrogen atoms were located at the south pole, and some could also be found at the north pole. Two hydrogen atoms, together with an oxygen atom, make up a water molecule. Thus, it was concluded that the hydrogen was really an indicator of large amounts of water ice at the south pole. Together with the radar results from the Clementine mission, the case for water on the Moon seemed quite solid.

Water on the Moon was more than just a scientific curiosity. It also represented a resource that could be used by future space missions.

Turn of the Century

The Lunar Prospector mission reignited interest in the Moon among space planners and the general public. Its results seemed to provide a fitting close to the century that had given birth to spaceflight. The rise of a new millennium seemed to be a cue for a new age of space exploration, but also heralded the close of this brief, but interesting, second wave of Moon missions.

No flights to the Moon would take off for a few years. But plans for greater achievements were developing within space agencies in various countries. It was time to consider the next steps, and how to achieve them.

Lunar Prospector approaches the Moon   NASA/ Boris Rabin

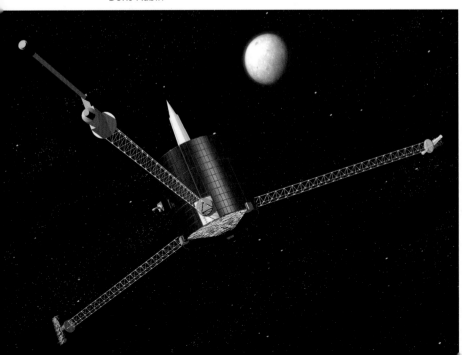

6 Water on the Moon

When the Apollo astronauts returned Moon rocks to Earth, scientists were amazed to find that they were essentially devoid of water. Minerals on Earth normally have a measurable water content, even when they appear to be totally solid. Water enters rocks through pores, and is also sometimes formed or trapped when the rock first forms.

Early astronomers had observed dark patches on the Moon and called them 'seas', believing that the Moon held continents and seas like Earth. Modern astronomy quickly dispelled these notions, but scientists were still amazed at the true nature of lunar material.

There are no vast oceans, but there are also no lakes or rivers on the Moon. There is no atmospheric pressure to keep water in a liquid state. A cup of water, transported to the surface of the Moon, would instantly flash into water vapour and dissipate into space.

For decades, it seemed that the Moon was totally barren of water. This suggested that astronauts who went there would need to transport all their water supplies with them. Water is a heavy, bulky substance, and mission planners try to reduce the amount that is carried on space missions.

But spacecraft investigations have overturned this concept. The discovery of water on the Moon has been a profound breakthrough in the planning of lunar missions.

Falling Ice

Water is actually delivered to the Moon on a regular basis. It comes in meteorites and comets that strike the surface. The huge, cratered terrain that dominates photography of the Moon demonstrates this. But most of it doesn't stay. The heat and pressure of impact turns the water into vapour, and it quickly departs from the Moon, escaping into space. Astronomers sometimes spot brief flashes of light in dark areas of the Moon, and know they have seen another impact.

The Shadows

Most of the Moon is exposed to glaring, direct sunlight, unfiltered by an atmosphere. It bakes the surface and drives off any residual water-ice that could be left behind by an impact. Some water could survive for a few days on the Moon if it impacted on the night side. But because daylight lasts for two weeks, water-ice that's exposed on the surface, or even buried just below the ground, cannot survive.

The Moon has some areas in its polar regions where sunlight never shines. The rims of large craters act like walls shadowing their interiors from the Sun, for the Sun never rises high enough in the sky to shine directly into them.

It was thought that ice falling into these crater regions might survive.

Hypothetical illustration of ice close to the lunar surface   X Prize Foundation

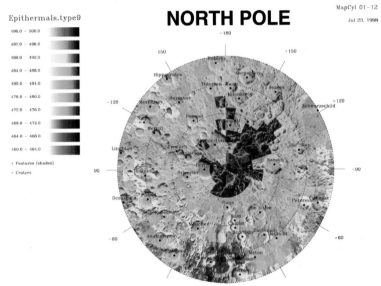

Neutron spectrometer map of Moon's north pole, indicating ice deposits   LANL/NASA

(Below) Neutron spectrometer map of Moon's south pole, indicating ice deposits   LANL/NASA

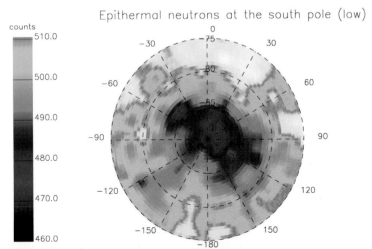

Sheltered from sunlight, it would experience freezing conditions, and remain solid. Ice might be blasted directly into the crater regions by impacts, or it could drift in as water vapour from impacts in nearby areas.

This theory seemed plausible. But there was no proof for decades, even after astronauts had landed on the Moon.

The dark nature of the polar terrain means that it is difficult to explore. Decent photography was lacking for years. The Clementine spacecraft (1994) was able to generate pictures of the region using radar pulse technology, which works better in low light than a camera, and allowed the poles to be mapped in detail. Craters that had the right topography to serve as ice traps were identified. Clementine also performed radar experiments that suggested water could be trapped in some of these crater regions, but the evidence was not convincing. Some rocks and minerals can also reflect radar pulses in the same fashion.

Lunar Prospector (1998) settled the matter decisively. Results from its neutron spectrometer suggest that water-ice is located in fairly large quantities at the Moon's south pole, and to a lesser extent, at the north pole. Lunar Prospector couldn't spot the exact locations in great detail, but scientists could take a good guess. The shadowed craters identified in the Clementine images fall within the broad footprint identified by Lunar Prospector.

Lunar Prospector in orbit   NASA

Further Investigations

The belief that there is ice on the Moon is now settled. But it's barely understood. We don't know how much there is, or how deeply it is buried. Is the ice mixed up with lunar soil like frozen slush? Is it like snowballs buried in the soil? What minerals are dissolved in the water? We can't tell without going to the south pole and investigating more closely.

It's difficult to do this from orbit. Something has to land there. A polar lander could investigate the lunar ice with instruments placed on top of the soil (like spectrometers). It could also dig into the upper layers, and use drills to explore to a depth of several metres.

A roving vehicle could perform these activities at several different locations. This is important, as conditions could change over a distance of a few tens of metres. Microscopes and small chemical laboratories on board the lander would be used to examine the ice and the soil around it.

Digging the ice could prove to be difficult, even for a robot. In 2008, the NASA Phoenix spacecraft landed at a northern polar region of Mars, and began digging into the soil with a long robot arm. It found ice deposits just a few centimetres below the surface. Scooping the deeply frozen ice into the lander's digging shovel was tricky, due to its extreme hardness and its cohesive properties. Phoenix also experienced problems in tipping the icy soil into scientific instruments on board the lander. Ice on the Moon will probably be at an even lower temperature, and possibly even more difficult to handle. Designers of robot ice-samplers for the Moon will need to account for these problems.

Penetrators and Impactors

Penetrators are another way to investigate lunar ice. They bury themselves deep in the surface, and can then explore the ground. Impactors could be fired from an orbiter in polar orbit. Unlike penetrators,

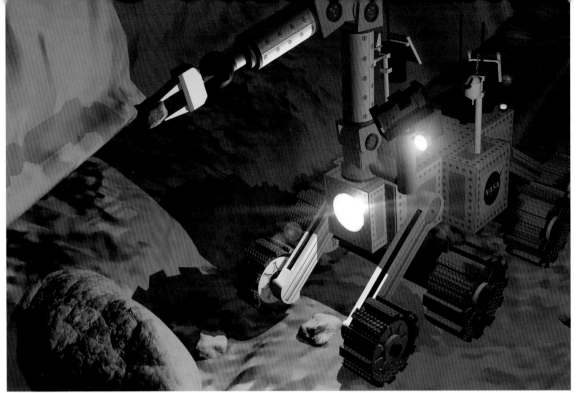

Hypothetical NASA robot investigates a polar region on the Moon   NASA

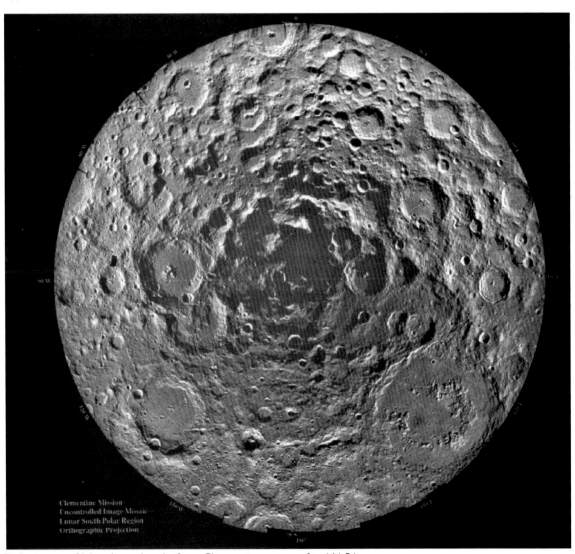

Radar image of Moon's south pole, from Clementine spacecraft   NASA

THE NEW MOON RACE

however, they are not designed to function after their hard landing.

A crude way of checking for lunar ice was practised by the Lunar Prospector spacecraft at the end of its mission. With its fuel running out, and its mapping mission complete, controllers decided to deliberately crash the spacecraft into the Moon's south pole. Astronomers on Earth turned their telescopes on the region, hoping to spot the impact. If the spacecraft landed in a huge patch of ice, some of this might be blown upwards as water vapour. This could be spotted by optical spectrometers tuned to the light emissions of water vapour.

Lunar Prospector did not generate any water vapour clouds. But this wasn't a major blow to the theory. It merely showed that not every region at the poles is an oasis.

This technique of using a spacecraft as an impactor will be practised on future lunar missions.

Ice Sample Return

At some point, a robot spacecraft could be launched to return an undisturbed sample of lunar ice to Earth. But this would be difficult. Getting a spacecraft back from the Moon is hard enough, and the lunar ice samples would need to be carefully protected during their journey. They would require refrigeration and protection against shock.

Alternatively, the ice could be melted into water and returned. But this would destroy some of its properties. It would probably not be worthwhile to transport such a sample all the way back to Earth.

In the near future, it seems that

Radar image of Moon's north pole, from Clementine spacecraft NASA

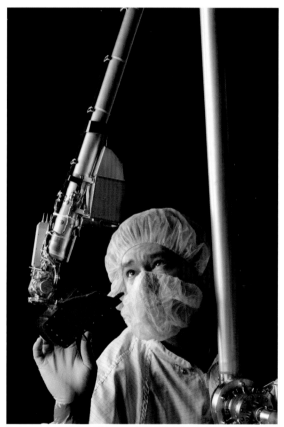

Robot arm of the Phoenix Mars lander   University of Arizona/NASA/JPL

analysis of the lunar ice would best be performed on the Moon itself.

Using the Ice

The discovery of ice on the Moon

is useful to scientists. Some of this material, like comets in general, could contain ancient materials that date back to the formation of the Solar System and have remained undisturbed and unchanged for eons.

But spaceflight planners have other reasons to celebrate the discovery of water on the Moon. It could also be used to help people to live there.

Water is essential to life. Drinking, cooking and hygiene are obvious uses. If astronauts are to live on the Moon in large numbers, for extended periods, it could be cheaper to use water that's already there than to transport it all the way from Earth.

Water can also be broken down to make oxygen. Again, another vital substance could be found locally, instead of imported.

Hydrogen and oxygen, the two gases released when water is broken down, can also be used as rocket fuel. Spacecraft returning to Earth from the Moon could utilise this.

Mining the Water

Nobody really knows how the ice would be mined or transported. The methods will depend on the depth and distribution of the ice, as well as the technology available. Robots with large scoops, similar to excavators on construction sites, could extract the soil, then load it into processing equipment in which the water could be extracted (probably using heat to turn it into vapour), then recondensed into pure ice.

It's been suggested that a future lunar base should be located at the south pole itself, where it will be close to the water. But water could be transported elsewhere on the Moon. Small spacecraft could make short, sub-orbital 'hops' by firing rocket motors, and land close to other bases. Transporting the ice overland, using rovers, is also possible. But the long distances and rough terrain could make these journeys difficult.

Ice from the Moon could even be sent far off the Moon itself. It's possible that lunar water could be transported to space stations in Earth orbit or elsewhere in space. The Moon's gravity is fairly low, and it takes less energy to transport something from the surface of the Moon into near-Earth space than from the Earth itself. Lunar water could even be used by spacecraft heading to Mars and beyond.

Water and Glass

In 2008, a surprising discovery was made in lunar samples from the Apollo 15 mission, which landed in 1971. Small beads of volcanic glass were found to contain traces of water which had been sealed inside when the glass had cooled from a liquid state. The amount of water found was minuscule, but it challenged the long-standing assumption that the non-polar regions of the Moon were totally devoid of water. However, although it's unclear whether water-bearing volcanic minerals are common on the Moon, they would seem to be an unlikely source of useful quantities of water.

SMART-1 spacecraft heads for the Moon   ESA

7 The New Fleet

After years of quiet planning, a new fleet of probes is returning to the Moon. During the gap of several years that elapsed between the Lunar Prospector mission of 1998 and the next probe, there was plenty of time for digesting the results of the last missions, and working out how to go further in our investigations.

SMART-1
The European Space Agency (ESA) is one of the world's top space powers. Its contributing nations have developed powerful rockets and sent advanced probes to the planets. Surprisingly, ESA was relatively slow to send a mission to the Moon, and its first mission was relatively modest. ESA actually sent a spacecraft to Mars before it launched anything to this nearer target.

SMART-1 was a small test spacecraft that represented another 'indirect' way of exploring the Moon. The primary goal of this mission was to test new technology (SMART is an acronym for Small Missions for Advanced Research in Technology), but sending the spacecraft to the Moon allowed it to return scientific data. SMART-1

SMART-1 spacecraft stacked for launch   ESA

Graphical illustration of SMART-1 ion motor   ESA

into orbit. The body of the spacecraft was a box smaller than one metre on each side, with two solar panels.

SMART-1 tested an ion-propulsion system that uses electrically charged particles for thrust. This is a slow but very fuel-efficient way to send a spacecraft across large distances. It also used a careful sequence of gravitational tugs with the Moon to help it reach its target. Similar methods had been used before on the Hiten probe (1990) and the rescue of the HGS-1 communications satellite (1997).

The instruments carried by SMART-1 were experimental and miniaturised. Its main tool was a lightweight camera system that photographed the lunar surface. SMART-1 also made observations of the Moon's gravitational field. Subtle changes in the spacecraft's orbit were watched to identify regions on the Moon's surface with higher gravity. This technique has been used regularly by other lunar and planetary probes.

SMART-1 proved technologically successful, and also added some scientific results to its overall mission. It operated for roughly three years.

Kaguya

The second wave of lunar missions began with the tiny Japanese spacecraft Hiten. Japan had plans for a small follow-on mission, dubbed 'Lunar-A', that would have orbited the Moon. It was expected that this would launch in the mid-1990s. But technical problems produced delays in the spacecraft's launch, and the mission was eventually shelved.

was launched in 2003 as a piggyback payload on an ESA Ariane 5 rocket that placed a large communications satellite

Japan returned with a more ambitious spacecraft. The Kaguya orbiter, which lifted off in September 2007, represents Japan's first attempt at a true lunar exploration mission, and is one of the most sophisticated unmanned spacecraft ever sent to the Moon. Kaguya is a rectangular, boxy spacecraft, 4.8 metres long, by 2.1 metres wide, by 2.1 metres deep, launched by an H2A launch vehicle from southern Japan. Kaguya has a single solar panel and a large dish antenna on a boom. Its name derives from a princess in Japanese mythology.

Kaguya carries instruments to observe the surface of the Moon, study the particles and fields in the space around the Moon, and even observe the atmosphere of the Earth from its distant position.

Close-up of lunar surface from Kaguya   JAXA

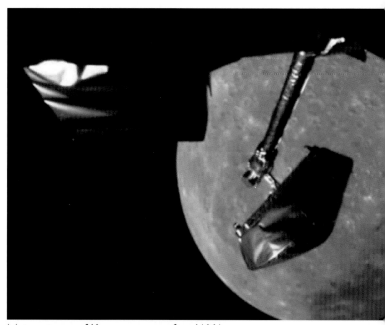
Main antenna of Kaguya spacecraft   JAXA

Kaguya spacecraft undergoes preparation for launch   JAXA

Earthrise seen by Kaguya   JAXA/NHK

Kaguya deploys its two sub-satellites in lunar orbit   JAXA

Magnetometer boom deployed from Kaguya   JAXA
(Below) Japanese tracking station   JAXA

As it arrived in lunar orbit, Kaguya deployed two small satellites into independent orbits. These transmit signals that are used to study charged particles around the Moon and the Moon's gravitational field. One satellite serves as a communications relay between Kaguya and Earth.

Kaguya also carries high-definition video cameras, still photography cameras and a laser altimeter to measure the landscape. Radar pulses can penetrate below the lunar surface to reveal underground structures.

Kaguya extended a long boom after reaching the Moon that holds a magnetometer. Placing the magnetometer which probes the Moon's weak magnetic field, away from the spacecraft's body ensures that it will not be disturbed by any magnetic fields in the spacecraft itself.

Kaguya settled into a final operational orbit roughly 100 kilometres above the lunar surface. It

42

has performed an extensive series of observations with no major technical glitches, and has even observed changes in the lunar surface caused by the Apollo 15 mission. Kaguya experienced no serious problems in its first year of operation, and was still working well in its second year.

One of Kaguya's most surprising discoveries is the apparent shortage of water-ice in a large crater at the Moon's south pole. This discovery did not rule out the possibility of finding water-ice on the Moon, but it did suggest that it would be less plentiful than earlier estimates had suggested, and highlighted the need for further exploration of the Moon's polar regions.

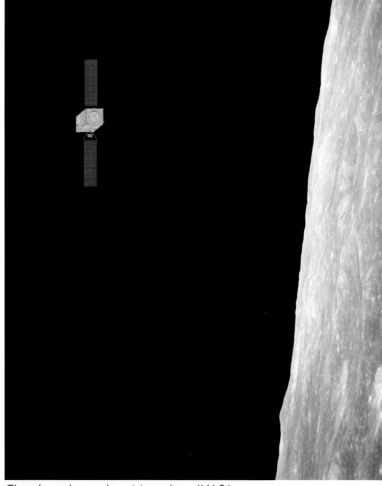

Chang'e-1 in lunar orbit   Morris Jones/NASA

Chang'e-1

China's space program has steadily advanced since its first satellite launch in 1970. In 2003, China became only the third nation on Earth to launch its own crew-carrying spacecraft. It is therefore unsurprising that China is sending robot spacecraft to the Moon.

China's debut lunar mission is Chang'e-1. The name is derived from Chang'e, a princess in a Chinese fairytale who consumed an elixir of immortality and was banished to the Moon.

Chang'e-1 is an orbiter carrying gamma-ray and X-ray spectrometers for mapping the chemistry of the lunar surface. It also sports a stereo camera system that can photograph the same patches of lunar terrain from different angles, which allows the construction of three-dimensional views of the surface.

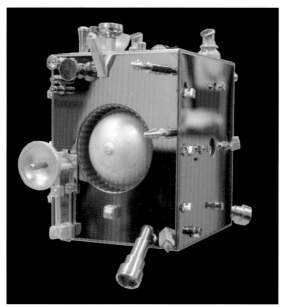

Chang'e-1 model with solar panels deleted   Morris Jones

Chang'e-1 has also photographed the Earth from deep space with an ultraviolet camera, and measured the solar wind. A microwave instrument on the spacecraft sends pulses that

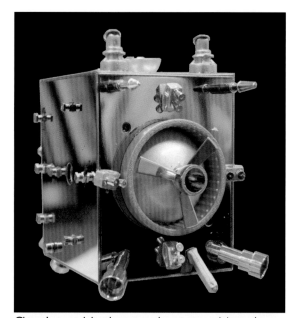

Chang'e-1 model with main rocket engine   Morris Jones

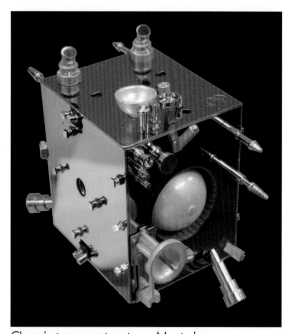

Chang'e-1 perspective view   Morris Jones

(Below) Chang'e-1 with solar panels extended   Morris Jones

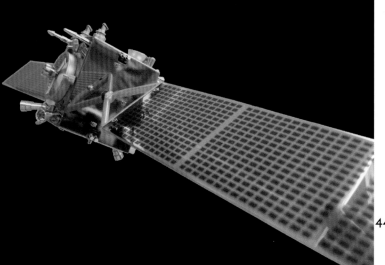

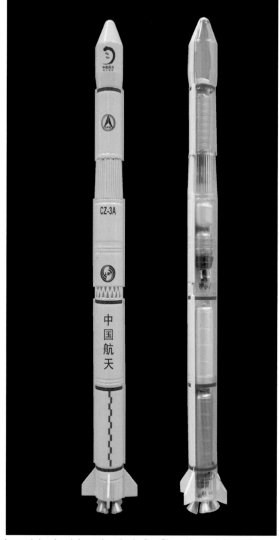

Long March 3A launch vehicle for Chang'e-1   Morris Jones

penetrate beneath the lunar surface, allowing measurements of the depth of the lunar soil.

The design of Chang'e-1 is based on a Chinese communications satellite, and resembles a box with huge solar-panel 'wings'. The body of the spacecraft is 2.2 metres long, by 2 metres wide, by 1.72 metres deep.

Apart from its scientific payload, Chang'e-1 carries recordings of Chinese patriotic songs and traditional tunes that were transmitted back to Earth from the Moon.

Chang'e-1 was launched by a Long

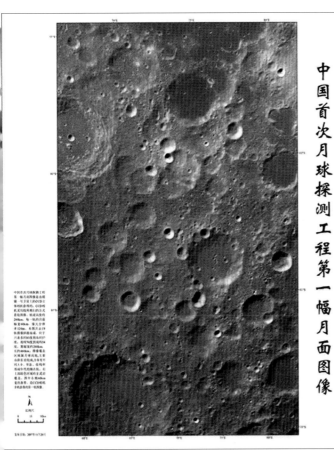

中國首次月球探測工程第一幅月面圖像

First picture released from Chang'e-1   CNSA/Permission granted through Chinese Consulate, Sydney

March 3A rocket from Xichang in October 2007, just weeks after the Japanese Kaguya probe. It arrived in lunar orbit in early November and orbits the Moon at an altitude of roughly 200 kilometres.

Chang'e-1 is being tracked by ground stations in China, and by antennas in Europe and Australia that are operated by the European Space Agency. Although China's lack of a large, globe-spanning tracking network means that other nations' antennas are needed to support the mission, no American tracking stations are working with Chang'e-1.

Chang'e-1 has performed well over an extended period, giving Chinese scientists the confidence to proceed with future lunar missions. The spacecraft was still functional more than a year after its launch.

Chandrayaan-1

India's space program has produced a robust fleet of domestically built satellites and a steadily improving stable of rockets. In recent years, India has demonstrated the ability to field rockets capable of sending probes into deep space. Lunar exploration is thus a logical target for a nation with a powerful launch vehicle and a sophisticated satellite capacity.

Chandrayaan-1 ('Moon Vehicle 1') is an orbiter with a side length of roughly 1.5 metres, and has a small solar panel. The spacecraft carries a large array of scientific instruments, including stereo cameras that can take images with a resolution of up to 5 metres. Various spectrometers will examine the chemical properties of the lunar soil. A small radar unit will map the ground, and a laser altimeter will

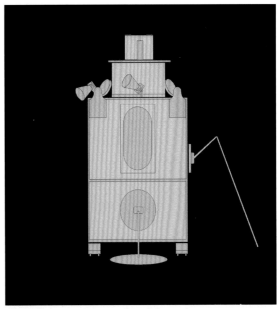

Chandrayaan-1 spacecraft   Morris Jones

Chandrayaan-1 in assembly   ISRO/ISAC

Upper instrument platform of Chandrayaan-1   ISRO/ISAC

(Below) Chandrayaan-1 after final assembly   ISRO/ISAC

Chandrayaan-1 in testing   ISRO/ISAC

Chandrayaan-1 X-ray spectrometer in preparation, from UK STFC(UK) ESA ISRO

Chandrayaan-1 X-ray spectrometer in detail   STFC(UK) ESA ISRO

(Below) M3 instrument for Chandrayaan-1, from USA   NASA/JPL

Polar Satellite Launch Vehicle for Chandrayaan-1   Thejes

(Below) Polar Satellite Launch Vehicle before launch   Thejes

Polar Satellite Launch Vehicle ignition   Thejes

measure terrain elevations. There is also a radiation sensor. Some of these instruments are supplied by foreign space agencies and laboratories. The advanced X-ray spectrometer carried on the spacecraft is a duplicate of an instrument originally flown on the European Smart-1 mission, built in the United Kingdom, which will detect metallic elements on the lunar surface.

NASA's Jet Propulsion Laboratory has supplied the moon mineralogy mapper, or M3 instrument, which is a

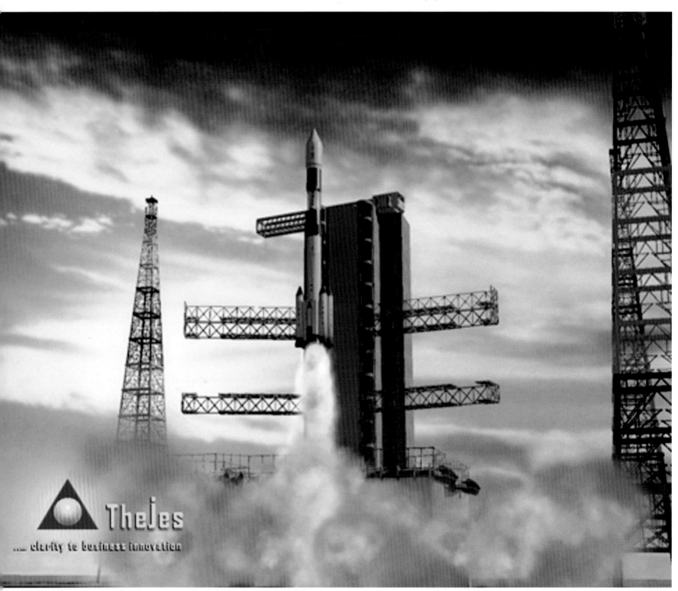

Polar Satellite Launch Vehicle liftoff   Thejes

THE NEW MOON RACE

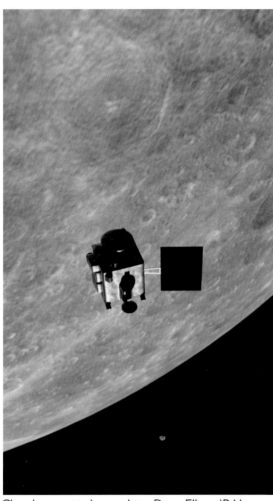

Chandrayaan-1 in lunar orbit   Doug Ellison/RAL

high-resolution spectrometer. Bulgaria is another international contributor to the Chandrayaan-1 project.

Chandrayaan-1 carries a Moon Impact Probe that will detach from the main orbiter, then fire a small rocket motor. This small box carries a camera and a radar system that measures the distance between the probe and the lunar surface. The probe will make increasingly close observations of the lunar surface as it descends, before being destroyed on impact. A similar mission profile was flown by the US Ranger spacecraft in the 1960s.

Chandrayaan-1 was launched in October 2008 by an Indian Polar Satellite Launch Vehicle, or PSLV. The PSLV is a medium-range rocket that is mostly used to launch satellites into polar Earth orbit (at right angles to the Equator, passing over the north and south poles). The mission is expected to last two years.

Chandrayaan-2 performs observations   Doug Ellison/RAL

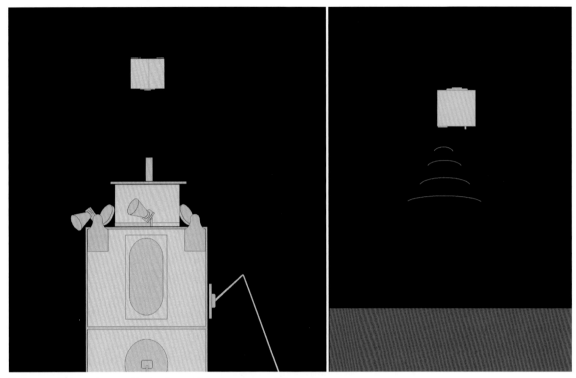

Release of Moon Impact Probe from Chandrayaan-1   Morris Jones

A New Moon Race?

It's interesting to realise that three of the current dedicated Moon missions have been produced by Asian nations. The spaceflight prowess of China, Japan and India matches the current strength of their economies. Japan has been heavily industrialised for several decades, while China and India have experienced explosive economic growth in recent years. Gaining a foothold in space is consistent with the overall rise of these nations. But some would speculate that, in a low-key fashion, a new 'Moon race' has emerged between these nations. The original 'space race' between the United States and the Soviet Union was largely a product of geopolitical rivalries and military tensions. Similar conditions are developing around Asia, as industries boom, military capabilities expand and strategic tensions rise. Today's lunar missions can still be used as propaganda tools and demonstrations of strength.

8 America's Twin Probes

Two American robot probes scheduled for launch in 2009 round off the latest wave of robot lunar exploration. America's past record of lunar exploration is extensive, and is unmatched by any other space power. Understandably, the next NASA missions to the Moon will deliver results that go beyond what is currently known, and set the scene for more ambitious missions to follow.

The Launch
The next two NASA spacecraft to fly to the Moon will be launched together, on the same rocket. An Atlas V 401 launch vehicle has been slated to blast off in the first half of 2009. The Atlas V class of rockets has previously boosted spacecraft to Earth orbit and even to Mars. A similar Atlas V rocket was also used to launch the New Horizons mission to Pluto in 2006. The heavy capacity of this vehicle allows these two lunar spacecraft to fly on a single launch.

Lunar Reconnaissance Orbiter
The primary spacecraft in this planned twin launch is the Lunar Reconnaissance Orbiter (LRO). In some ways, its instruments and mission are typical of the current fleet of lunar spacecraft. LRO is boxy in shape, comparable in size to its international counterparts, with a single solar panel and a dish antenna on a mast. It carries

Atlas V launch, similar to planned launch of Lunar Reconnaissance Orbiter   NASA

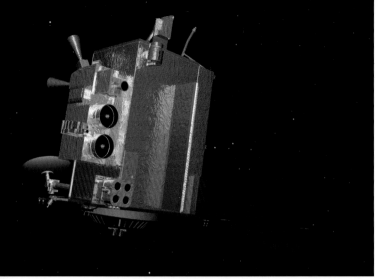

Lunar Reconnaissance Orbiter with instrument
apertures   NASA

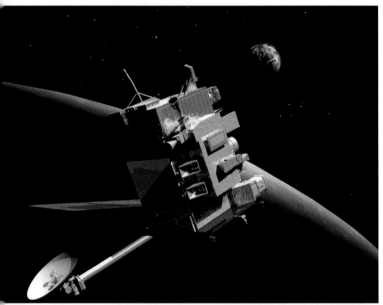

Lunar Reconnaissance Orbiter in lunar orbit   NASA

Lunar Reconnaissance Orbiter transmits to Earth   NASA

cameras and spectrometers, along with a laser altimeter. LRO is expected to function for at least a year in orbit.

LRO will observe the Moon in unprecedented detail. The spacecraft will be placed in a very low orbit, just 50 kilometres above the lunar surface. Most current orbiters fly at more than twice this altitude. This close approach to the lunar surface will allow its instruments to focus on smaller patches, increasing the resolution of most of its observations.

LRO's main camera will observe the Moon with a resolution comparable to spy satellites on Earth. Some imagery will be taken with each pixel covering just 50 centimetres. Mark Robinson, the principal investigator for the camera, claims that somewhere between 5 per cent and 10 per cent of the lunar surface will be photographed at this very high resolution. Some other areas will be photographed at 1 metre per pixel, which is also high resolution. Decisions on which areas will be photographed at the highest resolutions have not yet been made. The camera will probably photograph some of the Apollo landing sites, enabling the descent stages of the lunar modules that remained on the Moon to be identified.

The goal of this detailed photography is the production of highly accurate maps of the lunar terrain. A similar function was performed before the Apollo missions by the Lunar Orbiter spacecraft, but their cameras were not powerful enough to reveal detail on a fine scale.

Lunar Reconnaissance Orbiter in vibration testing   NASA/GSFC

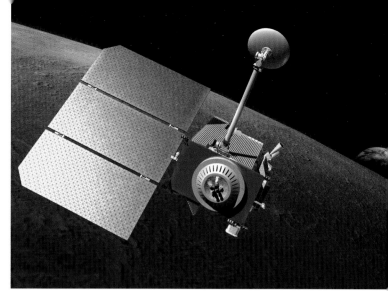

Lunar Reconaissance Orbiter scans the lunar surface   NASA

Lunar Reconnaissance Orbiter is lowered into a thermal vaccum chamber test   NASA/GSFC

Diviner infrared scanner from Lunar Reconnaissance Orbiter   UCLA

LRO's highly detailed images will certainly be scientifically productive. But the orbiter's main mission is more applied than theoretical. This spacecraft is designed to provide data necessary for astronauts to return to the Moon. Charting landing sites, regions of specific geological interest, and potential hazards, are all priorities.

LRO will map the surface temperatures of the Moon, which are highly variable. Lacking an atmosphere or liquid water, there is little to regulate the flow of heat during the two-week lunar day and the two-week lunar night. Certain regions could be more forgiving than others, owing to shadowing effects or the thermal properties of their rocks and soil. Finding such environments could be useful for stationing long-term expeditions in the future. An infrared scanner known as 'Diviner' will carry out these measurements.

Photography from LRO will be compared to images taken by the Apollo missions. The goal is to chart any changes in the surface (mainly from meteorite impacts) that could have occurred in the decades since these earlier images were taken. The Moon is constantly bombarded by meteorites, but establishing a rate of fall has never been done with any accuracy. Scientifically, this will be interesting, but the main goal of the exercise will be to gauge safety levels for future explorers. High-resolution imagery will be useful for identifying small impacts, which are probably numerous.

LRO also carries a radiation monitoring experiment.

LRO at the Poles

Observing the Moon's polar regions has been of prime interest to recent missions. While it's now certain that there is water-ice trapped in the permanently shadowed regions, little is known about it, so LRO has polar investigations as another area of priority. An ultraviolet camera will peer into these permanently shadowed regions, using weak reflections from starlight and other sources to reveal previously unseen areas. LRO's main camera will also repeatedly photograph the polar regions at different times, revealing which areas are permanently shadowed, which areas experience light and darkness, and which areas are perpetually bathed in sunlight. The latter are particularly interesting. Scientists have speculated that, somewhere at the poles, there could lurk a mountain that will be dubbed the 'Peak of Eternal Light'. This would tower over the surrounding polar terrain, catching the sun perpetually. Any equipment placed in such a region could depend on a reliable supply of solar energy. Again, the benefits to future explorers are obvious.

LRO will also refine the search for water-ice, defining its locations more precisely. A neutron detector and the ultraviolet camera will both contribute to this search. Until now, spectrometers have been able to tell that there is water somewhere inside a broad region being scanned, but have been unable to tell exactly which parts of the field of view contain it. Knowing exactly where the water is will permit future missions to extract it. LRO also carries a small radar imaging system that will help with this search.

LCROSS: Making a Big Splash

The final stage of the Atlas V rocket that launches the Lunar Reconnaissance Orbiter will also fly to the Moon. It will be 'shepherded' there by a second spacecraft, riding just beneath the LRO in the Atlas V

LCROSS is boosted to the Moon   NASA

(Below) LCROSS with attached rocket stage approaches the Moon   NASA

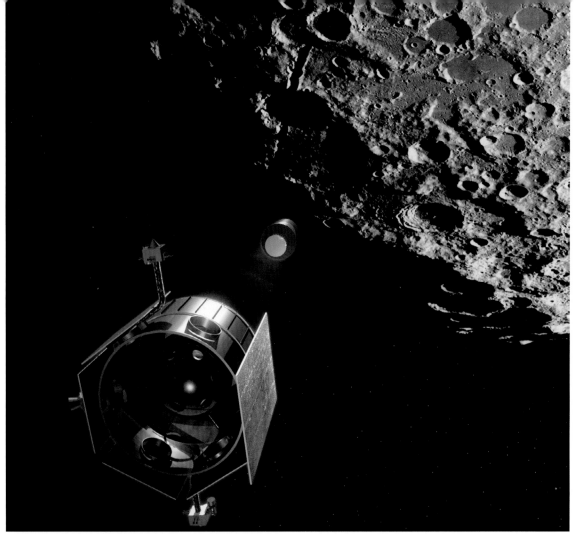

LCROSS spacecraft releases its rocket stage   NASA

LCROSS observes the impact of its rocket stage   NASA

Cameras and sensors for LCROSS   Northrop Grumman

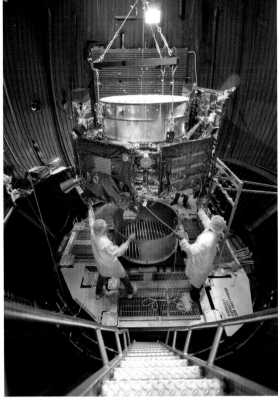
LCROSS undergoes testing   NASA/Northrop Grumman

payload fairing.

LCROSS, or Lunar Crater Observation and Sensing Satellite, is a simple spacecraft that will remain clamped to the rocket stage for most of its flight. It's a short, stubby cylinder with solar panels bolted to its side. For roughly 80 days after launch, LCROSS will steer the rocket stage like a tugboat through a large Earth orbit until it is ready to complete its short but enlightening mission.

LCROSS will send the Atlas V stage into an area near the south pole of the Moon, producing a huge explosion of surface material that should be visible to telescopes on Earth. Debris is expected to be thrown almost 50 kilometres high. LCROSS will also watch this impact closely with its own cameras and instruments. This is not the first time that a rocket stage or spacecraft has been steered to a controlled impact, but none have previously been able

to generate a visible plume of debris. With the benefit of precise targeting, and better maps of the lunar ice, LCROSS will try to achieve this goal. The Atlas V rocket stage will also leave behind an artificial crater, which will be visible long after the plume has fallen away. But LCROSS itself will not last much longer. Roughly ten minutes after the impact of the rocket, LCROSS will also plunge to the lunar surface, producing a second, but less dramatic, impact.

The Ultimate Lunar Map

At the end of LRO's primary mission, analysts will process its data to produce the ultimate lunar map, a map which will accurately chart the terrain and elevation of the Moon in extreme detail. It will include significant additional information. Assessments of the safety of various regions will be made by examining the roughness of the terrain, slopes and other topographical features. This will be used to map certain areas as safe landing zones for future missions. The illustration on page 58 is a demonstration of the mapping system, showing how safe zones will be mapped onto a regular contour map.

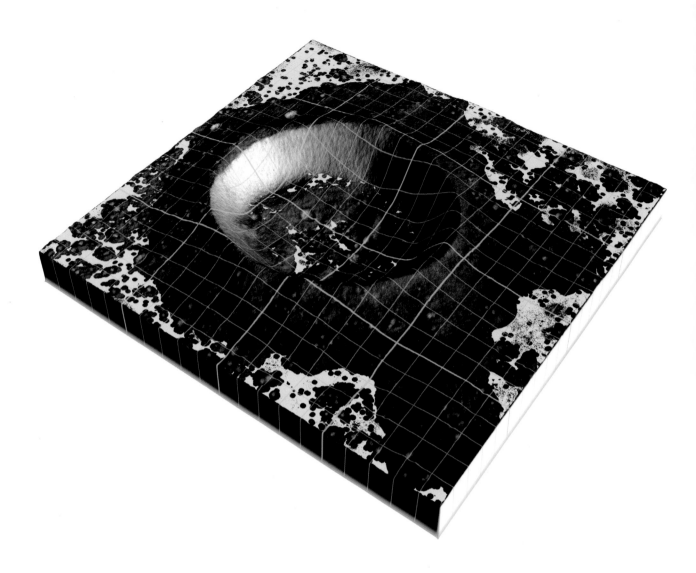

Simulated lunar terrain map. Safe landing sites are green. NASA/Goddard Scientific Visualization Studio

The green areas are judged to be flat and relatively free of debris that could damage a landing spacecraft. These maps will be computerised, allowing safe zones to be switched on and off over the regular mapping details. The processing power of the computers and the expertise of analysts on the ground are just as critical to the success of the mission as the spacecraft itself.

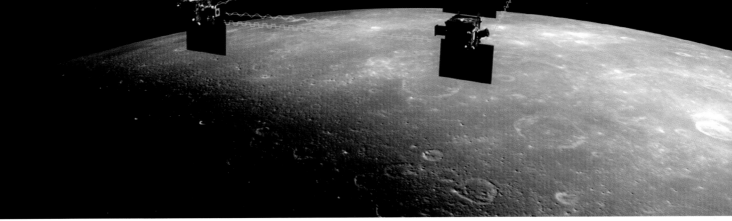

Twin GRAIL spacecraft in lunar orbit   NASA

9 America Continues

The launch of the Lunar Reconnaissance Orbiter and the LCROSS spacecraft on a tandem rocket ride in 2009 is a bold step in returning America to the Moon. And mission planning in the United States continues apace, with NASA drawing plans for new robot probes that will launch after 2010. These missions will address scientific questions that haven't been well covered by any previous lunar exploration.

GRAIL Mission
The surface of the Moon can be easily mapped from orbit, because there's no atmosphere to obscure the view. But probing the interior of the Moon is more difficult—we still don't have a detailed understanding of the composition of the Moon's interior. Finding out how the structure of the Moon differs from that of the Earth is critical to understanding how these two worlds formed in parallel. If the Moon was born from the collision of a Mars-sized object with the early Earth, as scientists seem to think, this fact will be reflected in the type of material found deep within it.

Scientists have used twin satellites in Earth orbit to make very precise gravitational maps of our planet. The satellites fly in formation, but watch for slight differences in their positions with radio beams. Any gravitational bulges beneath them will cause them to move differently.

Delta 2 launch vehicle, used here for a Mars mission
NASA/JSC

stations on Earth. This will permit very precise observations of the positions of both satellites. Gravity measurements with pixels of roughly 30 kilometres on the surface are expected.

Gravitational studies of the Moon have been performed by other satellites, but the precision of GRAIL will surpass all other observations. This will be the first mission launched specifically to examine the Moon's gravitational field. The precise monitoring of changes in the motion of two satellites in synchronised trajectories is the main factor in improving the accuracy of the measurements.

Apart from the scientific importance of the data that GRAIL will return, precise gravitational maps of the Moon will also help future spacecraft to navigate there. Apollo missions in orbit around the Moon were frequently diverted by 'mascons', or mass concentrations of rock lurking beneath the surface. These altered local gravitational fields, causing the spacecraft to deviate from their expected orbits. No Apollo mission was seriously affected by these problems, but it highlighted the fact that the Moon was uncharted territory. A precise gravitational map, coupled with the precise terrain maps from the Lunar Reconnaissance Orbiter, will make orbiting and landing on the Moon much easier.

LADEE
A smaller and less sophisticated mission is expected to be launched in roughly

A similar technique will soon be used at the Moon by the GRAIL mission, or Gravity Recovery and Interior Laboratory. It will fly on a Delta 2 rocket, a reliable but less powerful rocket than the Atlas V used to launch the Lunar Reconnaissance Orbiter.

GRAIL consists of two essentially identical satellites that will fly in formation, constantly beaming signals between each other and ground

THE NEW MOON RACE

LADEE spacecraft   NASA

the same timeframe as GRAIL. This spacecraft, which is an orbiter, is called LADEE, or Lunar Atmosphere and Dust Environment Explorer. LADEE is expected to launch on a Minotaur V rocket, a new, lightweight launch vehicle with five solid-fuel stages.

The Moon has essentially no atmosphere, but small traces of gases do exist on its surface. Some gas samples were collected in containers by the Apollo astronauts and returned to Earth. Gases such as argon and helium seem to be present close to the surface, but otherwise the Moon's atmosphere is poorly understood. Other gases could well be found at different altitudes from the lunar surface.

The Moon may lack air, but it obviously has no shortage of dust. Some scientists think that dust itself could make up a large proportion of the atmosphere. Dust can levitate when it is electrically charged, and it is thought that it could rise and fall from the surface of the Moon. Other orbiters will investigate this suspected floating dust, but LADEE will focus on it more specifically.

LADEE will orbit the Moon for roughly a month while its instruments are calibrated, then begin a 100-day mission of taking observations from a low orbit.

The main framework for the LADEE spacecraft is a simplified structure known as the Modular Common Bus (MCB), a basic spacecraft design that can be adapted for a variety of missions, which will fly for the first time on this mission. The instruments and equipment added to the Bus are changed for different spacecraft. The MCB could also be adapted to serve as a small lunar lander in the future.

Synergy

It is possible that both GRAIL and LADEE will be orbiting the Moon simultaneously for a large part of their missions. The gravitational field of the Moon and its atmosphere might seem to be two distinct areas for observation, but the two missions could prove that relationships exist between them. In recent years, astronomers have begun to popularise the theory that the Moon is not as seismically dead as we previously thought. Observations of 'bright patches', that flare up suddenly and disappear within minutes, are commonly reported. It's possible that some of these are caused by small meteorite impacts, but other theories are also gaining ground. Some scientists think that seismic disturbances in the Moon cause it to release pockets of gas, like volcanic outbursts. These events could also cause the ground beneath and around them to shift. Monitoring gases, dust and the gravitational state of the Moon at the same time could yield insight into events such as this.

It will also be interesting to see if any areas on the Moon experience changes in their gravitational fields over time. Twin satellites in Earth orbit have been able to spot gravitational changes caused by shifts in polar ice caps. Are

there movements inside the Moon? Gas outbursts could be one cause, but there could even be regions of molten rock deep inside the Moon, as there are inside Earth. Will we be able to see them shift?

Observations of the Moon performed by other spacecraft could also add to these missions. The 2008 Lunar Reconnaissance Orbiter will be long past its primary mission by the time the GRAIL and LADEE missions fly, and it is unclear if it will be available to take observations simultaneously with these two spacecraft. But areas of geological interest could be photographed by LRO, and later compared with recorded areas of activity. Gradually, overlapping sets of data would combine to build up a complete picture of activity within the Moon.

Before and After

The Moon's gravitational state is unlikely to change much in the future, apart from small transient events, but its atmosphere could possibly undergo massive changes. Scientists are concerned that future missions landing on the Moon, both robotic and manned, will contaminate the currently pristine lunar environment. The amount of gas produced by rocket motors and the venting of spacecraft cabins is fairly small, but it's enough to substantially increase the incredibly small amount of gas that is naturally present on the Moon.

Scientists want to perform studies of the lunar atmosphere, which include the LADEE mission, before such

Hypothetical lunar sample return-mission   NASA

contamination appears. Thus there is a need to fly this mission as quickly as possible. Future robot probes to the Moon could also contribute to studies of its atmosphere before it is too strongly influenced by large-scale exploration.

American Student Moon Orbiter

In 2008, calls for participation went out for the American Student Moon Orbiter, a small spacecraft to be launched in the near future. The scientific instruments for this mission will largely be drawn from American universities and colleges. The mission is designed to provide an apprenticeship project for upcoming young space engineers and scientists. At the time

of writing, the instruments and design of this mission have not yet been determined, but launch is expected at some time beyond 2010.

American Robot Sample Return

America has never launched a robot sample-return mission to the Moon, relying on the Apollo missions to retrieve samples. However, calls for such a mission, targeting an area not visited by the Apollo astronauts, are growing stronger from the American scientific community. The most likely candidate for examination is a region known as the South Pole-Aitken Basin, a large area that holds unique geological properties, including the possible exposure of rocks

Sample Return Capsule for Stardust mission   NASA

from beneath the Moon's crust. No spacecraft has yet landed in this region. A sample-return mission would not launch before 2013, and it is not clear when it would receive official funding. The design of the spacecraft is not resolved, but it could use a sample return capsule similar to the 1999 Stardust spacecraft, a US sample-return mission that collected dust samples from the comet Wild 2 and returned in 2006.

Funding Problems and Delays

In late 2008, NASA made a decision to supply additional funds to the Mars Science Laboratory, a large robot rover designed to explore the surface of Mars. The Mars Science Laboratory had experienced massive overruns in its cost, and faced cancellation if extra money could not be found to launch it. Scientists cheered the rescue of this complex mission, but braced themselves for the consequences, for the extra funding would be generated by taking money away from other space missions. At the time of writing, it was not clear how this would influence American plans for exploring the Moon, but the GRAIL and LADEE missions were potential targets for budget cuts, facing possible delays or cancellation. It was originally expected that both these missions would launch in 2011, but the funding dilemma could force a delay of several years. Even if GRAIL and LADEE are cancelled, it is possible they could be restored under a new round of mission funding in a few years. Scientific interest in flying these missions is strong, and it seems more likely than not that they will fly at some point.

Plans for the American Student Moon Orbiter are at an early stage, and there is currently no approval for flying a Moon sample-return mission. It is not clear if this mission will also be influenced by the cost dilemmas facing NASA.

10 Asia's Next Moves

The array of Asian missions that heralded the debut of the new Moon race was impressive, and more are planned. The momentum for a sustained lunar exploration program is strong across all the Asian space nations, and others will join the race in the future.

China Returns Quickly

China's Chang'e-1 mission has been an outstanding scientific and technological success. The performance of this

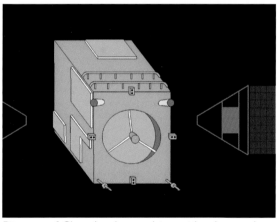

Diagram of Chang'e-2 lunar orbiter, with solar panels detached   Morris Jones

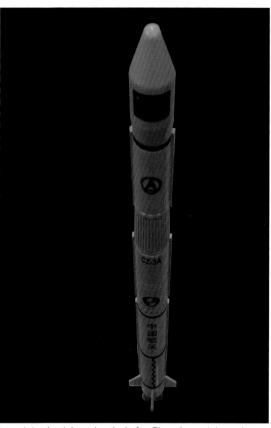

Long March 3A launch vehicle for Chang'e-2   Morris Jones

(Below) Diagram of Chinese lunar lander with hypothetical rover   Morris Jones

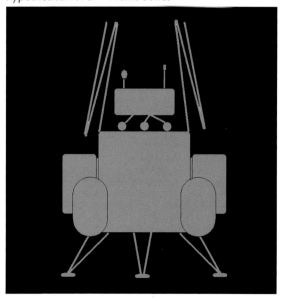

orbiter has given confidence to the Chinese space program, and paved the way for more advanced projects to follow. Originally, China did not announce plans for a new lunar mission in the short term, but this quickly changed in late 2007.

Shortly before the Chang'e-1 spacecraft was launched, China revealed that a duplicate orbiter had been assembled, which could have been launched as a replacement if Chang'e-1 failed. After Chang'e-1 had completed the first phases of its mission, China announced that the back-up spacecraft would be launched as a follow-up. Liftoff is expected in late 2009 or 2010. The mission will probably be dubbed Chang'e-2.

The Chang'e-2 spacecraft will carry a different overall set of instruments to Chang'e-1, but some instruments such as the stereo cameras will probably be replicated and flown again. Chang'e-2 could be placed in a different type of orbit, or targeted to explore regions that were not fully examined by the Chang'e-1 mission. China has announced that the mission will fly a different trajectory to the Moon, which will be less fuel efficient but more direct than the trajectory flown by Chang'e-1. Chang'e-1 seems to have used its fuel more sparingly than mission controllers had expected, so the next mission can afford to use more.

The second orbiter will use the same type of Long March 3A launch vehicle as the first. Apart from its scientific return, the mission will also give more experience in managing a mission in deep space to China's scientists and engineers, which will prove essential for the nation's future lunar plans.

Chinese Landings

Long before Chang'e-1 was launched, China announced plans for robot landers on the Moon. The first mission, which will probably blast off in 2013, is expected to place a rover on the surface. Around 2020, China hopes to launch a robot sample-return mission. The rover mission is difficult to describe accurately, owing to the limited information so far released, and some inconsistencies in what has been circulated.

Crude computer-generated images

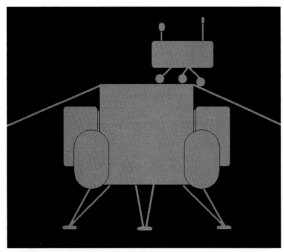

Chinese lander deploys ramps for rover   Morris Jones

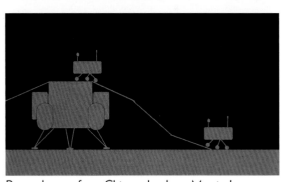

Rover departs from Chinese lander   Morris Jones

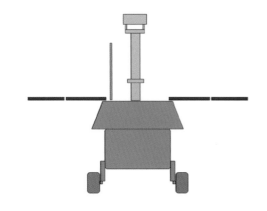

Possible design of Chinese lunar rover   Morris Jones

THE NEW MOON RACE

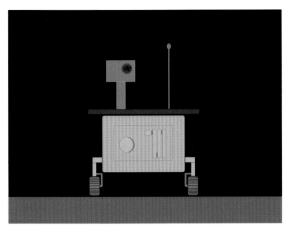

Possible design of Chinese microrover   Morris Jones

and animations of unmanned lunar landers, with footpads and boxy bodies, have been drawn up and circulated at aerospace exhibitions, and some have appeared in Internet forums and websites. Some of these early Chinese illustrations depict a lunar rover that seems to be a replica of the tiny Sojourner Mars rover, landed by NASA's Mars Pathfinder mission in 1997. The rover was shown driving down a ramp from the landing stage. This could simply be an early design, or a hypothetical rover invented by a graphic artist. Chinese engineers have demonstrated 'microrovers', roughly the size of a small microwave oven, in science exhibits, but it is not clear if these demonstration rovers have been integrated into any actual lunar projects.

Chinese scientists have tested a larger robot rover that strongly resembles the NASA Mars exploration rovers, shopping trolley-sized vehicles that landed in 2004, conducting the tests in sandy, rocky regions that simulate the lunar surface. Photographs of a similar rover prototype, displayed in an indoor testing facility, have circulated extensively in Chinese news outlets.

These larger rovers bear no resemblance to the tiny rover shown in the earlier computer-generated artwork. Again, it is unclear if the real rover, when it eventually flies, will look anything like them, but statements in the Chinese media suggest that it will probably be an evolved version of these prototypes. It will have six wheels, a body covered in reflective gold foil, solar panels that will fold outwards from its top, and a mast for a stereo camera system. A robot arm for placing instruments and tools on Moon rocks is included. The most recent prototype rover stands 1.5 metres high. China could decide to shrink the rover if weight limitations for the launch prohibit the landing of such a large vehicle. No discussion or exhibition of the landing stage appeared in these media demonstrations, but it could be similar to the one depicted in earlier graphics.

The rover would probably be strapped to the top of the lunar landing stage, like the Russian Lunokhod rovers before it. The landing stage would then extend ramps to allow the rover to drive off.

China has apparently sought cooperation with other nations to supply scientific instruments for the rover, but it is not known if any will be provided. China has previously obtained instruments from Europe for its scientific satellites, and European laboratories could continue this practice for its lunar program.

China has not supplied much information on any planned lunar experiments, but scientists have disclosed that a small radio astronomy experiment is being considered. Two radio receivers would be carried: one on the landing stage, and one on the rover. Using a technique known as interferometry, readings from both these instruments, which will be separated by some distance after the rover drives away, can be compared and combined to make better observations than a single instrument. Another instrument under consideration is a small optical telescope.

Disclosure of information about a Chinese lunar sample-return mission

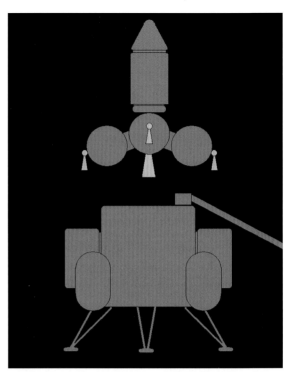

Chinese lunar sample-return stage lifts off   Morris Jones

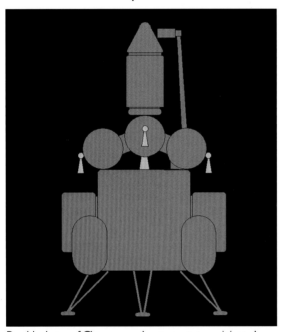

Possible design of Chinese sample return-mission   Morris Jones

has taken a different path to the rover mission. Illustrations and models of a sample-return mission, resembling a modified version of the Soviet Union's Luna sample-return spacecraft from the 1970s, started to appear in 2006,

as part of the collection of computer graphics of the earlier landing mission that showed a small rover. At the time, it was not clear if this was simply an artist's impression of the mission, or a real design. More recent events suggest that the pictures of the sample-return mission could be more accurate than the earliest rover pictures. In late 2007, a large model of the sample return mission was exhibited in China, with an almost identical design to these illustrations. This suggests that the design will remain consistent in the actual vehicle.

The sample-return mission is portrayed as a short, stubby rocket that sits atop a lunar landing vehicle. The lander is identical to the one depicted in the earliest rover landing missions, which suggests that China is developing a common landing stage for all its surface missions.

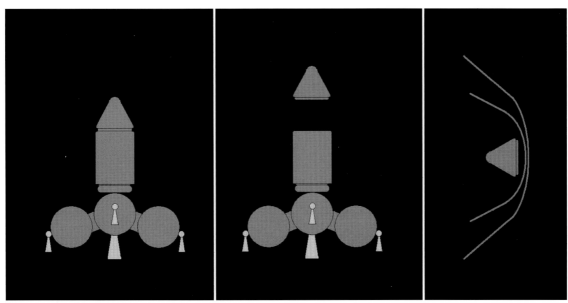

Chinese sample-return capsule arrives at Earth   Morris Jones

A robot arm on the landing stage drills samples from the lunar soil, then swivels upwards to place the samples inside a small conical capsule atop the rocket. The arm swings away, allowing the rocket to take off. Spherical fuel tanks at the base of the rocket would provide enough power to lift it out of the Moon's weak gravity and send it back to Earth. As it approached Earth's atmosphere, the conical sample capsule would detach from the rocket and re-enter, similar to an Apollo capsule from the 1960s. The capsule would parachute back to a landing in China.

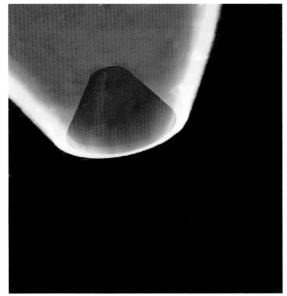

Chinese sample-return capsule during re-entry   NASA/ Morris Jones

Rockets for Chinese Landings

Originally, it was expected that both Moon landers would be launched by a new Chinese heavy-lift vehicle currently under development. The Long March 5 rockets, which will be the most powerful boosters China has ever flown, are discussed in greater detail in chapter 14.

In late 2007, China's media reported that the Long March 3B launch vehicle, an existing rocket with a long design heritage, was also being considered. In suggesting that the Long March 3B was potentially more reliable than the Long March 5, the report was hinting that production problems were anticipated for the Long March 5. China could elect to delay flying its lander until the Long March 5 was ready, but the media statement indicated that China could want to stick fairly close to its timetable of a 2013 landing. In 2008, further

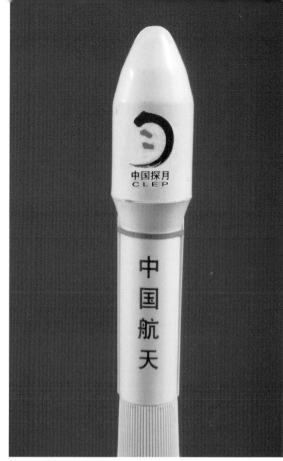

Payload fairing for Long March 3B   Morris Jones

Long March 3B launch vehicle   Morris Jones

Cutaway view of Long March 3B with lunar lander   Morris Jones

THE NEW MOON RACE

media statements cited 2014 as the expected year for the Long March 5 to make its debut, which is consistent with the previously announced switch of rockets for the lunar lander mission.

The Long March 3B is the most powerful of China's currently operational fleet of launch vehicles. It resembles the Long March 3A used to launch Chang'e-1, but features a larger payload fairing, slightly stretched fuel tanks, and four strap-on boosters around its first stage. Despite its power, the rocket is significantly less capable than a Long March 5. This could pose engineering problems for the mission.

So little information has been released on the proposed lander that it is difficult to know how much a change in launch vehicle would affect its design. It is possible that the landing stage designed to carry the rover would require no modification at all, but that the rover itself might be re-designed to reduce its mass, or that China might simply revert to the microrover of previous illustrations. Alternatively, the landing stage itself could be re-designed. China could also boost the power of the Long March 3B by adding a small rocket stage under the payload fairing, which would provide the final 'kick' to send the landing stage to the Moon.

No statements have yet been made concerning a change of launch vehicle for the sample-return mission. Presumably, China hopes that the Long March 5 will be ready by the time this mission is due to be launched. It is also probable that the sample-return craft cannot be shrunk as easily as the rover mission, and would be too heavy for a Long March 3B.

On the other hand, China could simply wait for the Long March 5 to be ready before either lander is launched. This would probably involve a slippage in the launch date for the first lander, but could eliminate the problems of shrinking the lander for a smaller rocket.

Japanese Lander

Japan announced plans for another lunar mission shortly after its Kaguya orbiter was launched in 2007. The new mission, currently referred to as 'Selene-2', will probably change its name shortly before launch. Selene-2 will land on the surface of the Moon, and is expected to launch around 2015 or soon afterwards.

Plans are still being defined. The Selene-2 mission could include one or two landers, and will probably carry a rover to the surface on at least one of them. The landing site of prime interest is the south pole of the Moon, but an equatorial landing site could be targeted by a second lander.

The mission's main goal will be the demonstration of Japanese technology for more advanced landers, but some scientific payloads will be carried, probably seismometers along with some type of spectrometer for inspecting the chemical composition of rocks. Methods of collecting samples, probably with mechanical arms, will be tested. The mission is also expected to deploy a small satellite into lunar

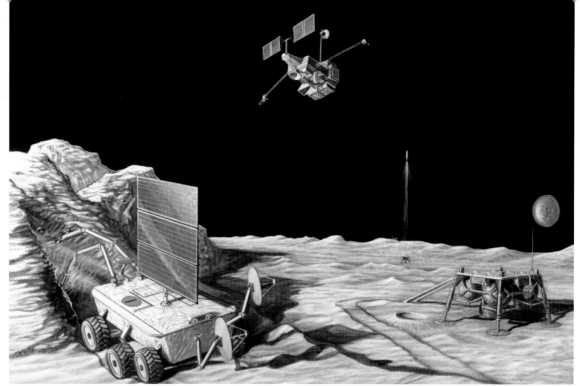

Japanese proposal for lunar orbiter, lander and rover   JAXA

Japanese rover prototype   JAXA

orbit as a communications relay, as did Kaguya.

Japan has experimented with lunar lander and lunar rover prototypes in the past. In fact, the original plan for the Kaguya mission called for it to release a small lunar lander after it reached orbit.

It was long expected that there would be a follow-on mission that would land, but planning ebbed and flowed.

It's not clear how this earlier work will influence the Selene-2 mission. Some of the landing technology will probably follow through, but Japan will probably

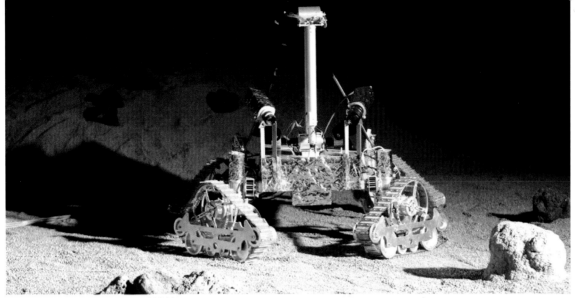

Japanese rover prototype   JAXA

Japanese H2A launch vehicle   JAXA

Inspection of H2A launch vehicle   JAXA

Japanese Aerospace Exploration Agency (JAXA) control centre   JAXA want to use a more sophisticated rover design. It's difficult to say what the rover will look like—the Japanese themselves seem unsure.

The launch vehicle to be used on the mission will probably be the H2A, the same rocket used to launch Kaguya.

Japan is also drawing plans for a larger lunar lander, dubbed 'Selene X', to be launched in the future. This could be a sample-return mission, or a test of robotics on the Moon. The exact mission and launch date are open to question at the present.

India Returns

Plans for future Indian missions were announced well before Chandrayaan-1, its first lunar probe, was launched. The second mission, called Chandrayaan-2, was announced as a combination orbiter/lander.

Official approval for Chandrayaan-2 was given soon after Chandrayaan-1 was launched in 2008, and before the spacecraft had even reached the Moon. Much to the amazement of some observers, India seems to be accelerating its lunar program. The mission had originally been tipped for launch around 2011, but officials now stated that Chandrayaan-2 would fly in late 2009 or 2010. The successful launch of the nation's first lunar mission seems to have provided the incentive for further achievements.

The details of the new mission were still being determined by Indian officials at the time of writing. The scientific instruments to be carried on Chandrayaan-2 would be selected on the basis of scientific data returned by Chandrayaan-1. Foreign instruments are expected to be carried alongside Indian instruments.

The mission will be launched by an Indian Geosynchronous Satellite Launch Vehicle (GSLV), which is more powerful than the rocket used to launch Chandrayaan-1 in 2008. The spacecraft would consist of a box-shaped orbiter, probably similar to the Chandrayaan-1 spacecraft, joined to a lunar landing platform. The lander would carry a

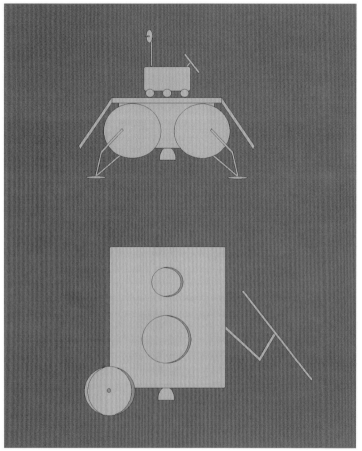

Chandrayaan-2 spacecraft   Morris Jones

THE NEW MOON RACE

Artist's impression of a future Indian lunar rover   Thejes

small rover. The exact design of the rover and lander are open to question, but some provisional artwork suggests the lander would be a four-legged structure.

The Chandrayaan-2 orbiter and lander would be placed into a highly elliptical Earth orbit by the launch vehicle, much like the Chandrayaan-1 mission. The orbiter would then fire its main engine to send the twin spacecraft on course for the Moon. Soon afterwards, the lander would detach from the orbiter, and the two vehicles would fly separately to the Moon.

The orbiter and lander would fire their main engines to enter orbit around the Moon. Later, the lander would fire its engine again to descend towards the lunar surface. Alternatively, the lander could make a direct descent to its landing site without entering orbit first.

The rover and landing platform are both expected to be built with

technical assistance from Russia, and both components of the flight would probably be built in Russia. It's possible that the rover will resemble a six-wheeled design that has been regularly exhibited by Russian scientists as a potential Mars rover. The 'Marsokhod' rover has never been launched on an actual mission, and Russia could use the Chandrayaan-2 mission as a chance to fly it.

India has announced no definitive plans for a follow-on to the Chandrayaan-2 mission, but a successful first landing could inspire the nation to send more missions. It is also possible that a similar landing stage or rover used on Chandrayaan-2 will be used by Russia on its own future lunar missions.

Shortly before the launch of Chandrayaan-1, Indian scientists remarked that proposals were being considered for a Chandrayaan-3 mission, although no official approval had been given for the spacecraft. The third Indian lunar mission would probably be a sample-return mission. It is unclear if this mission would use similar technology to Chandrayaan-2.

South Korean Lunar Plans

South Korea had made no announcements of lunar plans prior to the launch of the first Asian lunar missions. But this changed abruptly when China and Japan launched spacecraft to the Moon, and in November 2007 South Korea revealed its own plans for launching spacecraft there. The announcement seems to be a direct reaction to the activity taking place in other Asian nations, and reflects a desire to avoid being left behind as an emerging space power. KARI, the Korean Aerospace Research Institute, is the nation's space agency. A statement released on the KARI website openly admitted that the lunar missions were 'an ambitious plan ... to join Asia's space race'.

In the 1990s, South Korea launched its first satellites on foreign rockets. The nation also proceeded with the gradual development of a spaceport on its own territory, and the introduction of the Korean Satellite Launch Vehicle-1 (KSLV-1), an indigenous space-launch rocket made with a combination of Korean and foreign technology. Russia has been the principal outside source of expertise, and is responsible for developing the first stage of this two-stage rocket.

Prior to the lunar announcement, it was fair to say that Korea's space development plans were admirable, but modestly paced. The nation had mostly focused on launching practical satellites into Earth orbit, ranging from communications satellites to Earth observation satellites. Korea

Korean KSLV-1 launch vehicle   KARI

also launched an astronaut on board a Russian Soyuz spacecraft in early 2008, and has announced plans for training more astronauts, who would also fly on foreign spacecraft.

The Missions
KARI's plans call for South Korea to send an orbiter to the Moon by the year 2020, and to send a lander to the Moon by 2025. No precise details on the tasks to be performed by either mission have been announced, and no illustrations of either spacecraft published. The designs for the spacecraft and the overall mission plans have yet to be determined.

The Long Term
The long gap between the South Korean announcements and the proposed dates of the missions is noteworthy. It removes any pressure to deliver immediate results, and gives future governments the opportunity to change, delay or even cancel these plans. In the short term, the formation of plans at least satisfies calls for South Korea to join the Moon race.

Realistically, South Korea could probably not expect to fly a lunar mission from its own territory any sooner than 2020. Despite the advanced nature of their satellites, South Korea has yet to deploy a rocket capable of launching a substantial mission to the Moon. The KSLV-1 rocket is capable of placing small satellites in Earth orbit, and nothing else. The first KSLV-1 launch is slated for 2009, from South Korea's

Payload fairing for KSLV-1   KARI

Payload fairing for KSLV-1 opens   KARI

Second stage of KSLV-1   KARI

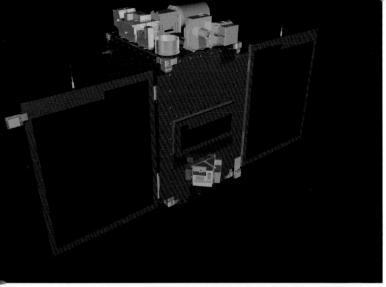

Korean Science and Technology Satellite   KARI

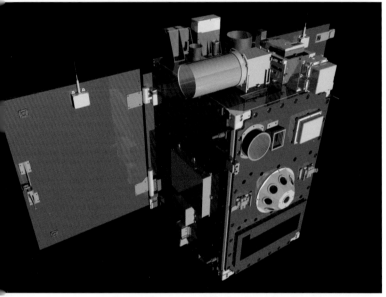

Korean Science and Technology Satellite, showing scientific payload   KARI

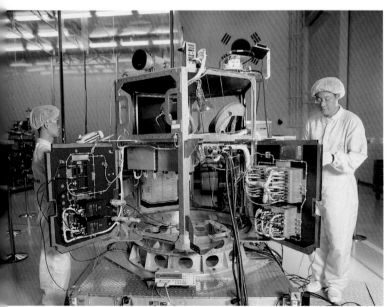

Korean satellite undergoing assembly   KARI

newly finished Naro Space Centre. Experience gained with this rocket will be critical to developing larger launch vehicles in the future.

Best Guesses

Assuming that South Korea's lunar plans survive the years ahead, what would they look like? Any outlines of these missions can be nothing more than speculation, but we can draw educated guesses from existing plans and technology.

A South Korean lunar orbiter could be based around one of the country's existing satellite platforms. The simplest case would be the Science and Technology Satellite design, a small, boxy spacecraft designed to carry a variety of scientific instruments. First flown in 2003, an upgraded version of this satellite will be the first test satellite launched by the KSLV-1 rocket. This satellite weighs a mere 100 kilograms, making it easy to send to the Moon.

Alternatively, authorities could elect to launch a high-resolution camera to make precise images and maps of the lunar surface. The Arirang-2 satellite, launched by South Korea on a Russian rocket in 2006, is an advanced spy satellite that can spot objects as small as a metre across on the surface of the Earth. A similar satellite, possibly with improved optoelectronics, could be sent to the Moon. High-resolution images of areas that were ignored by the NASA Lunar Reconnaissance Orbiter, or that require further study, could be useful.

South Korea is also working on

THE NEW MOON RACE

Arirang-2 satellite   KARI

a geostationary satellite that would be used for weather monitoring and communications. This large satellite could ultimately prove to be the best platform for a well-equipped lunar orbiter.

Guessing the design and mission of a South Korean lunar lander is more cryptic. A landing platform is a very different type of vehicle to an orbiting satellite. South Korea has unveiled a small experimental lander that may or may not be used on an actual mission. Once the lander touched down, what would it do? South Korea has an advanced capability in robotics, and it would seem logical to assume that a remote-controlled rover could be deployed. Alternatively, scientists could use its landing platform as an

astronomical observatory. Sample return is another option.

South Korea could make either or both missions narrowly focused, and target unresolved questions raised by earlier lunar missions. This could involve mysteries from the peculiar structures of a particular region to the distribution of a specific type of rare mineral, or the mapping of some sort of geophysical phenomenon such as moonquakes.

Both missions would be launched by the KSLV-2, a second-generation rocket that will boast more power than the KSLV-1. Details on the KSLV-2 are very sketchy at the present, and could change in the future, but it should be ready for flight by 2018. It will also presumably operate from the Naro Space Centre. A 2008 report from a KARI scientist claimed that the first lunar orbiter would be launched with an additional solid rocket stage placed atop the KSLV-2, which will boost the spacecraft beyond Earth orbit.

Beyond 2025

With South Korea's current lunar plans so vaguely defined, it's difficult to guess at any activities beyond 2025. It is possible that South Korea will not have launched its lunar lander by this date if technical, economic or political issues intervene. But South Korea (or a unified Korea) could find itself integrating its lunar plans more strongly with other nations, possibly supplying components for international lunar spacecraft. South Korea has not announced plans for developing a crew-carrying spacecraft, and it seems unrealistic to consider that this nation will send its own astronauts to the Moon in the foreseeable future.

Prototype for a small South Korean robot lunar lander.   KAIST

11 Other Nations, Other Missions

While Asia and the United States launch into extensive plans for lunar missions, other nations are quietly preparing to add their own contributions. Lunar exploration is truly becoming a global activity.

Russia's Next Mission

Despite its proud spaceflight heritage, Russia has not launched a mission to the Moon in decades. Russia's Federal Space Agency hopes to break this hiatus with a new mission dubbed Luna-Glob.

Luna-Glob is targeted for launch in 2012. The spacecraft is an orbiter that will fire a sequence of penetrators into the lunar surface. A penetrator is a projectile that impacts the ground at high speed and buries itself underground. They can be used to explore the rocks beneath the surface of a moon or planet, and also perform seismic experiments. Penetrators have long been proposed for lunar exploration, but they have never been flown before. A now-defunct Japanese lunar orbiter project called

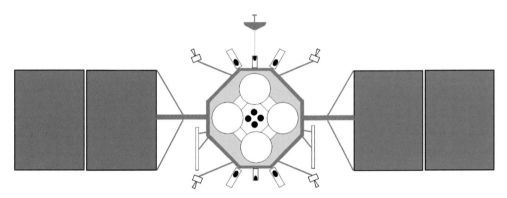

Luna-Glob spacecraft   Morris Jones

Large penetrator from Luna-Glob
Morris Jones

(Right) Launch of Luna-Glob
ESA/AOES Medialab

Lunar-A, proposed for launch in the 1990s, would have carried them. The penetrators on Luna-Glob will be used to create a network of seismic stations. Luna-Glob's collection of twelve small penetrators will be supplemented by a large penetrator that is essentially a small lunar lander. This large penetrator is expected to target the South Pole-Aitken Basin, a relatively unexplored region of the Moon.

Russia has plans for other missions to follow Luna-Glob in the near future. The Luna-Glob 2 mission would land softly on the surface of the Moon and deploy a rover, possibly near the south pole. Beyond this, Russia expects to launch another lander with a large rover, and possibly a robotic lunar sample-return mission. The mission plans are ambitious, but it remains to be seen if funding will be supplied in the long term.

British Microspacecraft
The United Kingdom has become a world leader in the development of 'microsatellites', or small, lightweight

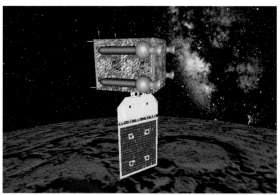

MoonLITE spacecraft   Surrey Satellite Technology Limited

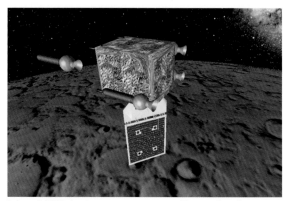

MoonLITE deploys a penetrator   Surrey Satellite Technology Limited

satellites, largely thanks to a team at the University of Surrey and its commercial offshoot, Surrey Satellite Technology Limited. Dozens of these tiny spacecraft have been launched into orbit, and it's only a matter of time

(Below) Penetrator decelerates for landing   Surrey Satellite Technology Limited

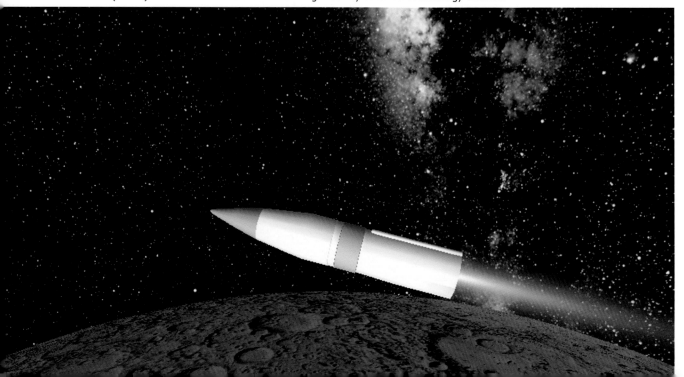

Penetrator over the south pole of the Moon   Surrey Satellite Technology Limited

before one reaches the Moon.

Britain is currently studying a microsatellite-based mission which could launch in the near future. This spacecraft is dubbed MoonLITE, or Moon Lightweight Interior and Telecom Experiment. The main spacecraft is a box-shaped orbiter with a small solar panel and a small collection of miniaturised instruments. Strapped to the exterior are four penetrators, similar to those to be carried by the Russian Luna-Glob mission. These would return seismic data from the Moon, but they would also measure the mineral compositions of rocks beneath the surface.

The use of a microsatellite would allow useful scientific exploration of the Moon to be performed at a moderate cost. But funding for the mission is far from certain, and an exact launch date has not been determined.

(Right) Penetrator impacts the lunar surface   JAXA

83

German Orbiter

Germany has made substantial contributions to spaceflight, both through its national space agency (DLR) and its membership of the European Space Agency. In the early twenty-first century, Germany drew its own plans for a lunar orbiter equipped with stereo cameras, spectrometers and radar, but in 2008 the plans were cancelled for financial reasons. It is possible that Germany could elect to fund this project in the future, possibly by working with other space agencies to help lower the cost.

MoonNext

The European Space Agency is investigating a lunar landing mission to be called MoonNext. The mission, to be launched by a Russian Soyuz rocket at some point between 2015 and 2018, would become the first European spacecraft to make a soft landing on the Moon. The exact design and instruments of MoonNext are still being determined, although it will probably carry seismic instruments and spectrometers. It will probably carry a small rover to move around the landing site. Other instruments and experiments will also fly, such as a radio astronomy package to test the Moon's suitability for observatories.

One potential landing site for MoonNext is Shackleton Crater, a large crater close to the Moon's south pole. The spacecraft will also test precision landing technologies that could be used for future missions to the Moon and Mars.

The launch date for the mission could slip if MoonNext fails to win funding in the near future.

Amateur Lunar Missions

Amateur radio enthusiasts have been building their own small satellites since the 1960s. These started out as small, unsophisticated radio transmitters that flew piggyback on regular satellite launches. Their original goal was to serve as radio relay satellites for amateur radio transmissions.

Gradually, these amateur satellites, or Amsats, have become highly sophisticated, and some have carried cameras and propulsion systems. They are like microsatellite missions, built on a smaller budget by teams of volunteers.

For some time, it has been suggested that an amateur satellite group could build a small lunar probe. This would be little more than a simple orbiter, with a minimal scientific payload—probably a camera, and possibly an experiment to measure radiation. The spacecraft would most likely ride piggyback on a satellite launch to the geostationary orbit belt, where most communications satellites are found. It would then use a small rocket motor to fly to the Moon.

No amateur lunar mission has yet been confirmed for flight, but it remains a possibility for the decades ahead.

12 The International Lunar Network

In the early twenty-first century, discussions within the space community settled on the need for a new project for lunar science. The International Lunar Network (ILN) will be a sequence of robot landers distributed across the surface of the Moon. The ILN will take simultaneous observations of the same types of phenomena across different locations, allowing a broad understanding of how certain events affect the Moon as a whole.

Network Science
The first lunar scientific network was placed by the Apollo missions. Scientific packages were left behind by all six missions that landed astronauts, and these continued to function long after the astronauts returned to Earth. Readings could be taken simultaneously from different locations. When a large object such as a meteorite struck the Moon, it could be measured by seismometers at different landing sites, allowing the readings to be compared. Today, the only Apollo experiments that still function are the laser reflectors, which require no power source. These are sophisticated prisms that reflect laser beams fired from Earth, and have allowed the precise

distance from the Earth to the Moon to be monitored and calibrated. The Apollo experiments demonstrated the value of placing experiment packages in different locations across the Moon, but no further networked landing experiments have been sent to the Moon since Apollo 17 flew in 1972.

The First Nodes
As on the Internet, individual points in the International Lunar Network are known as 'nodes'. The first node

Buzz Aldrin with lunar experiments on Apollo 11   NASA

85

Apollo laser reflector   NASA

missions to be principally dedicated to the ILN are to be launched by NASA. These will be two small robot landers, one sent to the Moon's north pole, and the other to the south pole. The significance of the poles as barely explored regions that could hold ice and other materials makes them attractive targets for landers.

The two polar landers will probably fly in 2013 or 2014. They could be launched together on a single rocket, or fly separately. Power for the landers could come from solar panels, but some polar sites will not have enough sunlight to generate power. NASA is investigating radioisotope power sources, which could be the preferred choice.

The landers will carry a small but carefully selected suite of instruments,

most of which will be duplicated on all the landers in the ILN. The exact instruments that will be common to the Network have yet to be determined, but scientists favour such instruments as laser reflectors, seismic monitors and heat-flow experiments, designed to monitor thermal changes in the lunar soil. Flying the same set of instruments on all the landers would allow different readings from different locations to be easily compared.

Some landers in the ILN may carry additional instruments. Some of these may appear on only one or two landers, and may be designed to provide some variation in the results. Particles and fields in the space immediately around the landers could be monitored. Some landers could carry materials science tests, or instruments that are specifically targeted at interesting features found at a particular landing site.

More Landers

The goal of the ILN project is to place six to eight small landers on the Moon in the years to follow the first landings. It is not clear where they will go, when they will fly, or who will launch them. NASA could launch two more nodes in the 2016 to 2017 timeframe, but this is not certain. If the project is to be truly international, other nations will need to fly their own nodes. The European Space Agency, the United Kingdom, Japan, South Korea, India and Russia have all expressed interest in contributing to the Network. Curiously, China does not seem to be involved in these discussions.

One way to distribute costs evenly could be to make future nodes multinational. One nation could build the landing spacecraft. Others could contribute instruments and components. Another nation could provide the launch. The Modular Common Bus, a basic spacecraft framework used on the US LADEE orbiter, could be used for the design of the US nodes in the network. Landing legs would be added to the outside of the framework to help it touch down and stay upright.

One obvious place for sending networked landers would be the far side of the Moon, a region that has not yet been visited. Communications with a lander on the far side would be potentially difficult, because there is no direct line of sight with Earth. NASA is investigating the possibility of launching a small communications satellite into orbit around the Moon, also based on the Modular Common Bus, that could serve as a relay between a lander on the far side and Earth.

Decisions

The format of the International Lunar Network is still being defined through meetings within space agencies, and between them. As a complex project, it will take some time for the details to be worked out. But the idea certainly has its merits, and support for it is clearly growing.

Some launches of nodes will probably slip beyond their originally announced dates, and there is a chance that the network will not grow beyond six landers. But this will still provide a valuable insight into the overall dynamics of the Moon.

Integration

Some previously announced lunar missions, such as the European MoonNext, Indian Chandrayaan-2 and Russian Luna-Glob 2 landers, could be designated as nodes in the ILN. This would produce overlap between missions specially dedicated to the ILN, such as the first two US landers, and the broader international fleet of lunar missions. Integrating these programs would magnify the scientific returns of the Network and the individual landers. Some of these missions are expected to land before the US nodes, meaning that the network could be considered active long before the United States stages its own landings.

13 Project Constellation: Return of the Astronauts

Humans have been absent from the Moon for more than three decades, but America has drawn up plans to return. Project Constellation is the official name for the development of a new set of rockets and spacecraft that will send astronauts into Earth orbit, take them to the Moon, and possibly carry them deeper into space. Project Constellation has been the result of changes in policy, and the necessity to upgrade America's human spaceflight capability.

The Big Gap
America's ageing Space Shuttle fleet will be retired soon, and NASA is scrambling to finish the assembly of the International Space Station before this happens. In the years that immediately follow, NASA faces the possibility of having no means to fly astronauts to the station with American spacecraft. Plans current in early 2008 called for astronauts to be launched on Russian Soyuz spacecraft. There is no replacement vehicle for the Shuttle that can be immediately pressed into service.

The need for a new US spacecraft has been apparent for years. Problems with the Shuttle have helped to propel the development of a new vehicle, which will bridge the gap between the International Space Station program and NASA's new plans.

NASA's potential imminent lack of a human spaceflight capability is reminiscent of the 1970s, when the Apollo program ended and the Space Shuttle was under development. US astronauts were grounded for almost six years, before the Shuttle finally flew. It is not clear how long they will have to wait during the next big gap.

Replacing the Shuttle with a new spacecraft called Orion is a major objective of the Constellation program, and its service in this role will be critical in the near future. However, its ultimate goal is to permit human spaceflight beyond Earth orbit, where the Shuttle itself was never designed to travel.

The Soyuz Dilemma
In early 2008, plans for the transition between the Space Shuttle program and the debut of the Orion spacecraft seemed to be generally resolved. The Shuttle would stop flying in 2010, and Orion would begin to carry astronauts around 2015, a gap of roughly five years. During the gap, US astronauts would ride to the International Space Station aboard Russian Soyuz vehicles, with the launch costs paid by the

US Government. This arrangement was somewhat embarrassing for the United States, which would be totally dependent on a foreign nation for this service. It also presented the possibility of price gouging, because Russia would have a monopoly on astronaut launches during this period. But the overall mood suggested that America was prepared to accept compromises in order to keep its astronauts flying.

By mid-2008, the situation had become more complex. US relations with Russia had rapidly deteriorated following Russian military incursion into South Ossetia, a disputed territory claimed by Georgia. Bellicose statements from Russia over the deployment of an American anti-ballistic missile radar system in Poland added to the problem.

Another strategic theatre added to the controversy. The US Government passed a law in 2000 that restricted commercial deals with nations assisting Iran with its nuclear development program. Russia has been a key supplier of nuclear infrastructure to Iran. Exemptions to this law had been made previously to allow the United States to purchase rides on Soyuz, given the importance of the vehicle to the International Space Station. But the ongoing development of a uranium enrichment program in Iran, coupled with the testing of long-range missiles, was strengthening opinion against suppliers to Iran.

The political and strategic concerns over Russia were by now enough to jeopardise plans to use Soyuz. How could America resolve the dilemma of losing access to the vehicle? Some analysts wondered if America would simply have to abandon the International Space Station for an extended period. It was suggested that the Space Shuttle could have its retirement delayed to keep the US crew-transport system to the station in operation. But that would have been technically complex, given the fact that contracts with suppliers were already being cancelled, and enormously expensive.

Soon afterwards, in late 2008, the world experienced the start of what seemed to be a massive financial crisis. Banks collapsed and stock markets fell. In the midst of this crisis, the US Government agreed to a massive financial bailout package, worth hundreds of billions of dollars, in order to stabilise the economy. During this turbulence, support for continued American use of Russian spacecraft was approved by the US Government, with little of the fuss or attention that had been previously expected. The Soyuz Dilemma had been resolved, but the concerns it raised highlighted the vulnerabilities in America's space infrastructure.

Talk of slightly delaying the retirement of the Shuttle was still active in late 2008, and some legislators were trying to prevent the destruction of infrastructure that would be needed for future missions. At the time of writing, it was not clear if this would actually lead to more flights, but the addition of only a couple of Shuttle launches would still leave a large gap to be filled by Soyuz missions.

A Work in Progress
Project Constellation involves the creation of a new crew-carrying spacecraft, a new fleet of rockets, hardware to carry astronauts to the Moon, and a tremendous amount of new infrastructure to support these vehicles. The introduction of these new launch facilities is already underway at NASA's principal launch site in Florida. This involves the demolition of old launch-pad structures to make way for new ones, and changes to the enormous Vehicle Assembly Building, a huge, boxy hangar that was used to stack the Saturn 5 rockets and the Space Shuttle.

Despite the bold pronouncements and beautiful pictures, Constellation must be regarded as a work in progress.

The design of everything from the rockets to the landers is constantly being revised. Any facts and figures published about the program could change in the years ahead, including the plans discussed here. Changes in the design of the spacecraft and rockets can already be detected between various illustrations supplied by NASA, and the illustrations here.

Constellation has been subject to heavy criticism since its inception, and the program will be subjected to technical and economic pressures in the years ahead. But Constellation's overall goals should remain consistent. America needs a new spacecraft and a new direction for its human spaceflight program.

Orion: The New Command Module
NASA is already developing a new capsule-style spacecraft to

Early mockup of Orion spacecraft   NASA/JSC

THE NEW MOON RACE

carry astronauts. Called Orion, the spacecraft is a conical vehicle with a hatch on its side, and a docking port at its tip. The resemblance to the Apollo command module is obvious. Orion will carry a cylindrical service module at its rear, containing fuel tanks, rocket motors and power systems. Again, this is strongly reminiscent of the service module carried by Apollo.

Orion will probably carry a crew of four astronauts on most missions, although some NASA documents speak of a crew capacity that could go as high as six for Earth orbital missions. Orion will be modified slightly for different missions and crew levels.

With 20 cubic metres of interior volume, the Orion capsule has two and a half times the room of Apollo, which held three astronauts and their supplies in only 5.9 cubic metres of space. The astronauts themselves will have roughly 11 cubic metres of free space to occupy.

The circular base of the Orion vehicle is 5 metres across, and the top will probably have an aerodynamic cap, designed to protect its hatch and docking system during launch. Like Apollo, there will be a small rocket placed on top of Orion to pull the spacecraft free of its rocket in an emergency.

The service module for Orion is of a different size to its Apollo counterpart, but the same general shape. It features a large rocket motor at its rear and a dish antenna for communications. Orion has two large solar panels for generating electricity, a departure from the fuel cells of Apollo and the Space

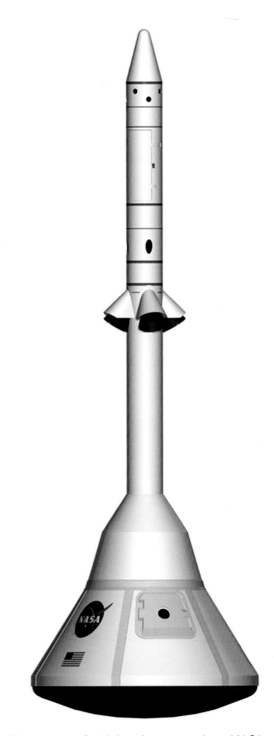

Orion spacecraft with launch escape rocket   NASA

Shuttle, which combine hydrogen and oxygen to generate electrical power. The service module will separate from the Orion spacecraft just before the spacecraft re-enters Earth's atmosphere, and will not be recovered.

Scale model of Orion is tested for water landings   NASA

Orion has already experienced numerous design reviews. Recent concerns have focused on ways of reducing its weight, but the overall conical shape should remain the same.

Early descriptions of Orion suggested that the spacecraft would descend to a parachute landing on solid ground, probably at a US Air Force base, with airbags or small rockets in its base cushioning its landing. But recent design reviews have suggested that a water landing could be used. Like Apollo, the spacecraft could land somewhere in the Pacific Ocean. It is not clear which landing option will eventually be used.

Orion will also feature advanced instrumentation and computer systems, moving beyond the technology used on the Space Shuttle. The capsule is also expected to be re-useable.

(Below) Orion spacecraft in lunar orbit   NASA/Lockheed Martin

It is interesting that NASA is returning to a conventional capsule design for its next spacecraft, rather than a winged shuttle-style vehicle.

First Flights for Orion

An unmanned Orion spacecraft is expected to make its first test flight in Earth orbit in 2014, although this could be revised. Later that year, NASA hopes to launch an Orion spacecraft with astronauts on board, but this also could slip. Afterwards, Orion spacecraft should begin making regular flights to the International Space Station, carrying crews and supplies.

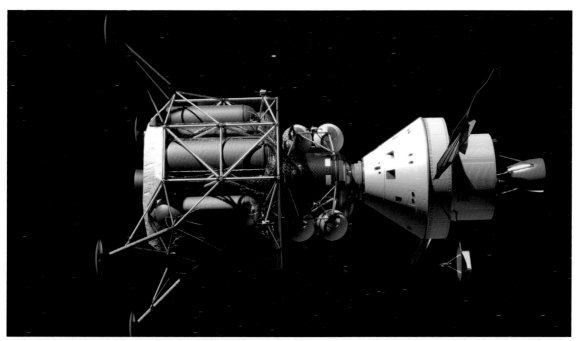

Orion spacecraft docked with Altair   NASA/JSC

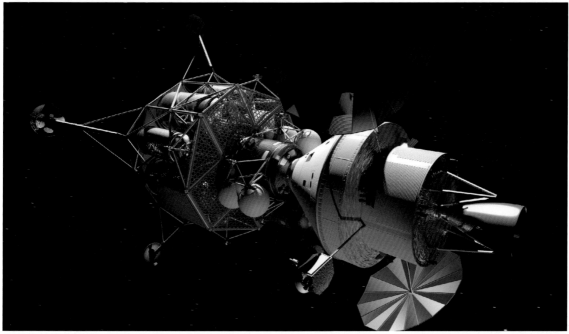

Orion spacecraft docked with Altair   NASA/JSC

Orion spacecraft and Altair prepare to depart from Earth orbit   NASA/MSFC

Altair: The New Lunar Module

Apollo flew to the Moon with two primary spacecraft: a command module, and a lunar module to land on the surface of the Moon. In parallel with the development of the Orion spacecraft, the Constellation Program is developing a new lunar module. This spacecraft is technically known as the Lunar Surface Access Module (LSAM), but is more commonly known as Altair.

As with the Orion spacecraft, Altair will be a much larger vehicle than its predecessor. But the overall design concept retains some of the principles of the Apollo lunar module. Altair will probably have room for all four astronauts who would fly on a Constellation lunar mission. On Apollo, two astronauts landed on the Moon while a third remained in lunar orbit to pilot the command module. The Orion spacecraft can operate automatically without any astronauts aboard.

The design of Altair is evolving, but it will feature four spider-like landing legs and a large descent stage containing rocket motors and fuel tanks. Sitting atop this will be an ascent stage, which is a pressurised cabin for the crew. When the astronauts leave the Moon, the ascent stage will take off using its own rocket motor, leaving the descent stage behind on the surface. The same overall design was used on Apollo.

Altair will probably include an airlock, enabling crew members to leave the vehicle while the main crew cabin remains pressurised. The Apollo lunar module barely had enough room for its two astronauts, and did not feature an airlock. The airlock will probably detach from the Altair ascent stage before it lifts off from the surface of the Moon.

New Rockets

A new fleet of rockets is being developed for Constellation, but final designs of the vehicles have not been entirely resolved. Just as Apollo had its Saturn rockets (principally the Saturn 1B and Saturn 5), the principal launch vehicles for Constellation will be dubbed the Ares 1 and Ares 5.

Ares 1 is the smaller of the proposed new rockets, with just enough power to launch the Orion spacecraft into Earth orbit. Ares 1 is a thin, two-stage vehicle that grows wider towards its top, giving it a strange appearance. The first stage of Ares 1 is like a stretched version of the Space Shuttle's solid-fuel rocket booster, using the same solid propellant segments as these boosters. Sitting atop this is a liquid-fuelled rocket stage,

Ares 1 rocket on launchpad   NASA/MSFC

Ares 1 launch   NASA/MSFC

Ares 1 ascent   NASA/MSFC

Ares 5 rocket on launchpad   NASA/MSFC

powered by liquid hydrogen and liquid oxygen. The Orion spacecraft sits atop this stage. In short, this is reminiscent of the Saturn 1B rocket's role in launching the Apollo command module on Earth-orbit missions, such as the Apollo 7 mission. Ares 1 stands 94 metres high in its current design, taller than the Space Shuttle stacked for launch.

Ares 5, like its Saturn 5 counterpart, is the larger of the two principal launch vehicles. Its first stage burns liquid hydrogen and liquid oxygen. Two stretched versions of the Space Shuttle's solid-fuel rocket boosters are strapped to its side. The lower assembly of this rocket is thus somewhat reminiscent of the Space Shuttle itself.

A smaller second stage, also burning liquid hydrogen and liquid oxygen, sits atop this. Finally, a large payload fairing encloses the spacecraft being launched by Ares 5. At 116 metres, this is just taller than the mighty Saturn 5 rockets of the Apollo program.

Unlike Saturn 5, the Ares 5 will not send astronauts to land on the Moon with a single rocket launch. Ares 5 will carry an Altair lunar module into Earth orbit. Later, an Orion spacecraft with astronauts aboard will be launched on the smaller Ares 1. The Orion spacecraft will rendezvous with the Altair, still attached to the second stage of the Ares 5, in Earth orbit, docking nose-to-nose. Then the second stage

THE NEW MOON RACE

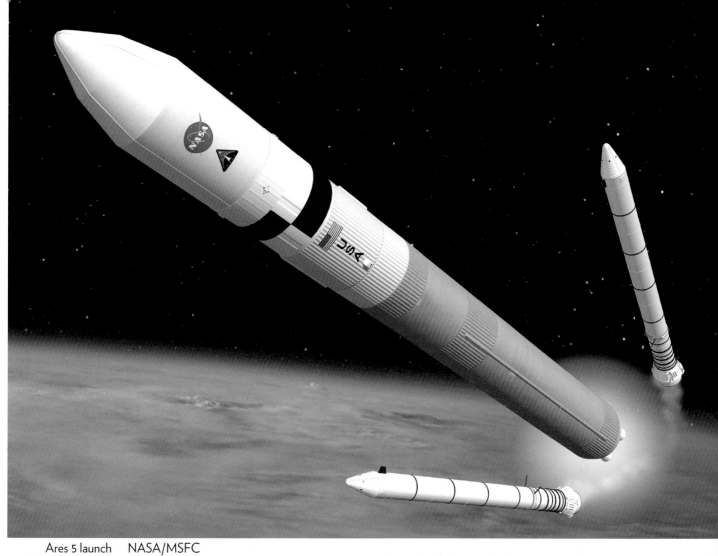

Ares 5 launch   NASA/MSFC

Ares 5 launch with Altair   NASA

PROJECT CONSTELLATION: RETURN OF THE ASTRONAUTS

Solid rocket booster segments for Ares vehicles   NASA

of the Ares 5 will ignite to send the two spacecraft to the Moon.

The docked Orion/Altair assembly would cruise to the Moon after separating from the final Ares 5 stage. Approaching the Moon, the Altair would fire its rocket motors to brake the joined spacecraft into lunar orbit. On Apollo, the job of braking into lunar orbit was performed by a large rocket motor at the rear of the command module (in the large cylindrical service module), not the lunar module.

The four astronauts would enter Altair and undock from the Orion spacecraft, which would orbit the Moon uncrewed. They would then descend to the lunar surface. Once lunar surface operations were completed, they would take off again in the ascent stage of Altair, and re-dock with Orion. They would then transfer to Orion, discard the Altair, and fly back to Earth.

Problems

Technical criticisms of Constellation hardware began as soon as the program was announced. More serious problems

(Below) Project Constellation lunar landing with Altair   NASA/JSC

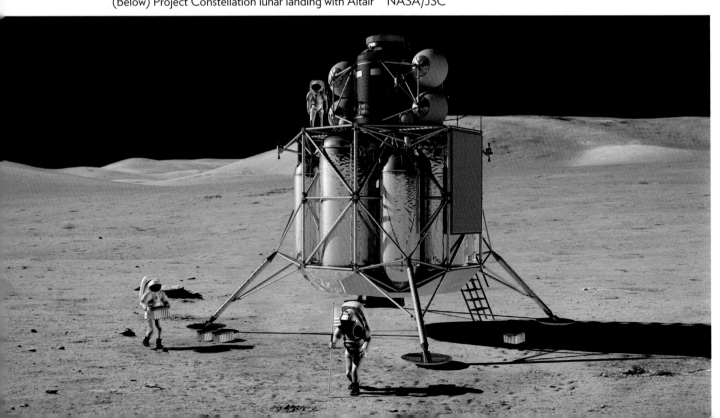

emerged as the design and testing of the Ares launch vehicles began. The Ares 1 rocket has come under heavy scrutiny for the vibration levels it will generate during launch. It is thought that these vibrations could be hazardous to the spacecraft and possibly its crew. Countermeasures designed to dampen launch vibrations have been proposed.

Some critics claim that the design of the rocket is so flawed that it should be shelved. They also point to its relatively modest lifting power, which is placing limitations on the mass of the Orion spacecraft it is designed to launch.

Alternatives

It is also possible that Orion spacecraft could be launched using some of the current fleet of American conventional launch vehicles, such as large Atlas or Delta rockets. At the present, such alternative vehicles do not appear in official plans, and they would only be able to send Orion into Earth orbit.

An alternative to Constellation, known as Direct, would scrap the Ares 1 rocket in favour of a new, heavier launch vehicle for Orion, with a design similar to the Ares 5. The Direct plan is highly controversial. Discussions of the Direct architecture circulate regularly on the Internet, and it has attracted a large group of followers. At the time of writing, NASA is not officially endorsing Direct, although the plans are rumoured to enjoy the unofficial support of some of its engineers.

Changes to the overall architecture and hardware of the Constellation program could appear in the future, if the technical problems of the current plans prove to be insurmountable, and if political factors intervene.

New Spacesuits

NASA is also commissioning new spacesuits for the Constellation

Prototype lunar spacesuit   NASA/JSC

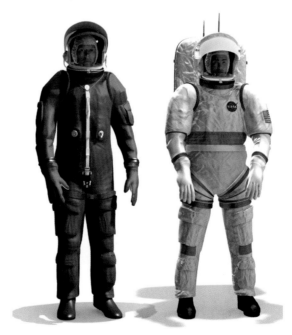

Constellation spacesuits for orbital spacewalks and moonwalks   NASA

program. Plans call for a lightweight spacesuit, to be worn by Orion crews on Earth-orbit missions, which can be used for spacewalking. A heavier suit, with a life-support backpack, will be used for walking on the Moon. The spacesuits are designed to be less cumbersome than the ones worn on Apollo missions, which greatly restricted the movements of the astronauts.

Landing on the Moon

NASA expects that the first human flight to the Moon in the Constellation program will not land astronauts there, just as Apollo 8 and Apollo 10 flew to the Moon without landing before Apollo 11's historic voyage. It is unclear how many orbital test missions would be made under Constellation. One plan would send an Orion spacecraft with an Altair lander to the Moon, and land the Altair without a crew on board. The Altair would later take off and rendezvous with the crewed Orion spacecraft in lunar orbit. Such a mission could take place in 2019.

The first human landing on the Moon since Apollo has been tipped for late 2019 or 2020 under the current Constellation plan. It is possible that this will change as the program adjusts to meet technical goals. Setting a precise year for a landing is difficult at such an early stage. It's worth remembering, however, that 2019 will be the fiftieth anniversary of the landing of Apollo 11, making it an attractive date to target.

Working on the Moon

The scene of the first Constellation lunar landings will probably bring back memories of Apollo. There will be ceremonies on the Moon, including the planting of the American flag. The astronauts will deploy experiments on the surface, similar to the actions of the Apollo astronauts. These experiment packages are currently being developed. Naturally, a lot of rocks will be collected.

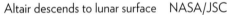

Altair descends to lunar surface   NASA/JSC

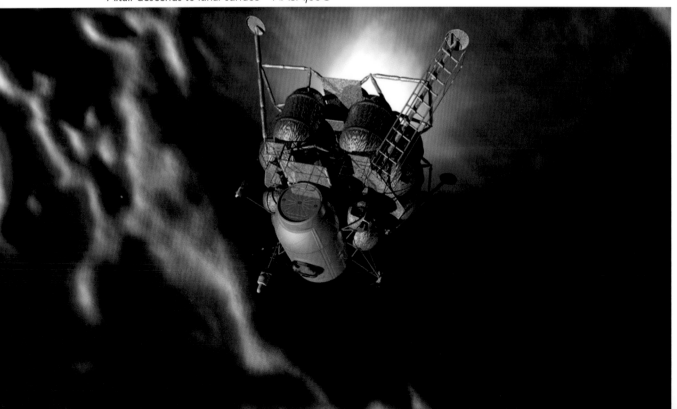

Altair lifts off from the lunar surface   NASA/JSC

Four astronauts will be on the Moon at the same time, with a larger lander and better equipment. It is not clear how long the first expedition will spend on the lunar surface, but much of the equipment they leave behind will continue to function for months, or even years. The scientific returns will be substantial.

The Constellation missions that follow will probably stay on the surface for intervals of up to seven days. But NASA will eventually work towards more sophisticated lunar expeditions.

New Rovers
NASA is examining the use of new lunar rovers on later Constellation

(Below) Astronauts with pressurised lunar rover   NASA

expeditions. Unlike the unpressurised vehicles used on Apollo, the Constellation rovers are expected to be large vehicles with pressurised crew cabins, which would allow the astronauts to cover large areas of territory over several days. The design of these rovers has yet to be determined. Some early designs feature spacesuits that plug into the exterior of the rovers. To make a moonwalk, an astronaut would simply climb into a spacesuit through a hatch in its back, then detach the suit from the outside of the rover.

Polar Expeditions

Some Constellation missions will be targeted at the polar regions of the Moon. Data from the lunar reconnaissance orbiter will help to select landing sites that are considered safe and interesting. This would permit detailed studies of lunar ice deposits, as well as the composition of these barely explored regions.

Lunar Base

Eventually, the Constellation program could lead to the construction of a small lunar base, possibly at the south pole. For this, timeframes and designs are very difficult to specify. The base would need to have an Altair spacecraft permanently stationed for an emergency return to Earth, plus an Orion spacecraft in lunar orbit to dock with it. The Altair lander could be modified to carry habitation modules and power systems, gradually building the base with several landings. NASA has dabbled with the development of inflatable habitation modules, but it is not clear if they will be used for the first lunar base.

The astronauts could experiment with extracting lunar ice for life support and other purposes. Stays of several months on the Moon would be feasible. Long-term missions to the Moon are seen as an essential part of preparing for manned missions into deeper space, such as expeditions to Mars.

International Missions

Constellation is primarily an American project. There has been a shift away from the heavy involvement of international partners demonstrated in the International Space Station

Hypothetical small lunar base   NASA

program, but this does not remove the possibility of multi-national participation in the future. Other nations will probably supply scientific expertise for Constellation, just as they did for Apollo. Non-American astronauts could fly to the International Space Station on some Orion missions to Earth orbit, and some may even reach the Moon. International politics, as well as domestic American politics, will strongly influence these decisions.

The Near Term

The near-term future of Constellation will probably be the most turbulent period of the entire program. The departure of the Bush Administration, which conceived the Constellation program, has presented the opportunity for revisions and possible budgetary attacks. Serious problems in the US economy, highlighted by the subprime mortgage crisis of 2008 and the bailing out of financial institutions by the government, have caused concerns among lawmakers, and the mood among taxpayers could also become hostile. Space exploration is an easy target for cuts in government spending. Funding cuts could produce changes in the overall design of the rockets and spacecraft, along with delays in the missions.

On the other hand, renewed support for Constellation could spring from the growing strength of foreign space programs, particularly China's manned spaceflight program. Challenges to US leadership in spaceflight could be enough to prompt higher funding levels.

As a long-term project, Constellation is potentially vulnerable to several cycles of government and economic upheavals. Its fortunes could vary from year to year.

Beyond the Moon

Some engineers are already envisaging the use of Constellation spacecraft for missions beyond the Moon. The most commonly discussed plan would fly an Orion spacecraft on a voyage of several months to a near-Earth asteroid. This mission would carry humans further into space than ever before, and would be highly demanding on the crew. It is not clear when, or if, such a mission would be flown.

14 China's Lunar Future

Of all the lunar ventures anticipated in the future, none are as occluded or as controversial as the plans of the People's Republic of China. China's obscurantism about its spaceflight activities is legendary. Secrecy abounds on many aspects of Chinese spaceflight, and access to facilities and personnel is heavily controlled. The nature of disclosure is reminiscent of the early Soviet space program, where grand results would be announced with a minimum of detail, and much information withheld. Several requests for the rights to images and other information for this chapter were placed with Chinese government officials, but none succeeded. Most of the images of Chinese rockets and spacecraft in this book are based on photographs of models, and on computer graphics. Three-dimensional renderings of the Shenzhou spacecraft were performed by Analytical Graphics Inc., a US-based aerospace software company that has studied the design of Shenzhou. Two photographs in this chapter were originally posted to the Internet by an anonymous source in 1999, apparently as an unofficial leak.

It is very difficult to speak of China's long-term plans for lunar exploration with any level of accuracy. In fact, it is most likely that the Chinese themselves have not yet prepared a definite long-term plan. This chapter explores some possibilities for long-term lunar exploration that are technically possible and make use of technology already available to Chinese space scientists.

New Rockets

A key element of China's future lunar missions is the development of a new generation of rockets. The existing Long March launch vehicles are powerful enough to send large spacecraft to Earth orbit, and medium-sized spacecraft (such as Chang'e-1) to orbit the Moon, but would seem to be insufficient for the heavy lunar spacecraft planned for the future.

China is currently developing a new modular rocket system, known as Long March 5, which offers major increases in launch capability. The power of the Long March 5 system can be changed by using different combinations of stages and booster rockets.

The Long March 5 series uses different fuel combinations to the current fleet of Long March rockets, which use hydrazine fuel and nitrogen tetroxide. These chemicals are stable liquids at room temperature, and are relatively easy to manage in a rocket's fuel tanks and piping. The next generation of Long March 5 rockets will use liquid oxygen and kerosene, or liquid oxygen and liquid hydrogen, depending on the rocket's configuration. Liquefied gases are far more difficult to manage, but they offer a substantial increase in power.

The Long March 5 rockets are physically larger than those in the current fleet. The rocket stages can be assembled in various combinations, including several rocket stages clustered together as boosters for the first stage. The diameter of the 'core' rocket, as well as the diameter of the boosters strapped to its side, changes in different versions.

China is also preparing to build a new spaceport. Chang'e-1 blasted off from a launch site in Xichang, on the Chinese mainland. But the next generation of Long March 5 rockets will take off from a site near the city of Wenchang on Hainan Island, which lies off the southern coast of China. This is closer to the Equator than Xichang or the other principal launch site at Jiuquan, where China's astronauts are launched. The construction of this new site was officially announced in September 2007. Work should be completed around 2012, according to current plans. Launches of the Long March 5 rockets should begin by 2014.

Stages for the Long March 5 rockets will be assembled on the Chinese mainland and transported to Hainan Island by ship.

A launch site close to the Equator gets a free 'kick' from the Earth's rotation, like a child sitting on the edge of a merry-go-round. Other launch sites also benefit from the Earth's rotation, but the higher the latitude, the less the benefit becomes. The European Space Agency operates a launch site in French Guiana in South America, which is also close to the Equator. For the same reason, most NASA launches take place from Florida, in the southern United States.

The combination of a new generation of powerful Long March rockets and a new launch site will give China a solid foundation for deep space exploration.

European Space Agency tracking station used to support Chang'e-1 mission   ESA

Robot Landings: Rovers and Sample Return

Plans for China's next robot missions were discussed earlier, in Chapter 10. Another lunar orbiter will fly in 2009. The first landing mission, which will probably blast off in 2013, is expected to place a rover on the Moon's surface. Around 2020 or slightly sooner, China hopes to launch a robot sample-return mission. At least one of these landers (sample-return type) is expected to use the aforementioned heavy-lift Long March 5 rockets, and will probably fly from the Wenchang launch site on Hainan Island. Landing on the Moon requires a spacecraft to carry a fairly large fuel load, as well as apparatus for the descent and touchdown. This adds to the weight of the spacecraft, which in turn demands more power from the rocket that launches it.

More Probes

China may decide to launch other orbiters to the Moon beyond Chang'e-2, scheduled for launch by 2010. A more advanced, next-generation Chinese orbiter could carry a different suite of instruments to Chang'e-1 and Chang'e-2. It could also fire penetrators at the surface. At the time of writing, no plans for a more advanced lunar orbiter had yet been announced. Such an orbiter could be heavier, and be launched from Hainan Island on the Long March 5 rocket.

Soviet robot lunar exploration was typified by repeat missions of the same type of spacecraft. Two robot rovers were landed on the Moon, and several attempts were made to launch sample-return missions. China could eventually fly other rovers to the Moon and other sample-return missions. These would probably use similar hardware to the first missions, but China could change some of the instruments. The missions would probably be sent to explore locations with different terrain and rock compositions to the first landing sites.

The development of a multi-purpose landing stage would also allow different sorts of missions to rover landings and sample-return. It is possible that a future Chinese lander could deploy a complex radio telescope on the Moon. The landing stage would touch down and unfurl a large dish antenna, probably resembling an open umbrella. This antenna could be used to explore frequencies blocked by Earth's atmosphere, or have its observations synchronised with other telescopes on Earth through interferometry. If China's first lander and rover carry an interferometry experiment, it could strengthen the case for more advanced interferometry missions.

China's Shenzhou Program

In 2003, China became the third nation on Earth to launch an astronaut on its own spacecraft. The spacecraft is known as Shenzhou, which is usually translated as 'Divine Vessel'. Four uncrewed test flights were performed before the spacecraft was considered safe to carry astronauts. The first uncrewed flight, Shenzhou 1, lifted off in 1999 and orbited the Earth for roughly one day. It returned to a soft

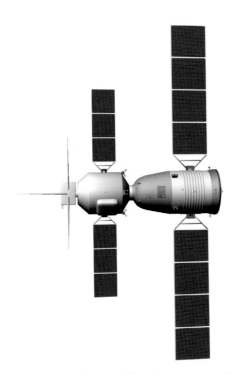

Computer simulation of Shenzhou spacecraft with antenna experiment assembly   STK

Detailed view of Shenzhou   AGI

Rear view of Shenzhou spacecraft   AGI

landing on the flat plains of Inner Mongolia, a northern Chinese territory. The AGI computer graphics of the Shenzhou spacecraft in this chapter

depict the Shenzhou 1 spacecraft on this historic mission. The collection of antennas at the front of the spacecraft was deleted on subsequent flights, and replaced with equipment such as cameras and microwave scanners. Future missions, depicted in other illustrations in this chapter, are expected to carry docking ports instead.

In 2003 the Shenzhou 5 spacecraft carried astronaut Yang Liwei into orbit for around a day. Roughly two years later, in 2005, China launched a second manned space mission, Shenzhou 6, which placed two astronauts in orbit for roughly five days. The Shenzhou 7 mission flew in 2008, and carried three astronauts aloft for three days. Shenzhou 7 also saw the first Chinese spacewalk.

All Shenzhou spacecraft to date

Forward view of Shenzhou   AGI

Crew patch for Chinese Shenzhou missions   Morris Jones

Spacecraft configuration for Shenzhou 5 mission, featuring a camera system   Morris Jones

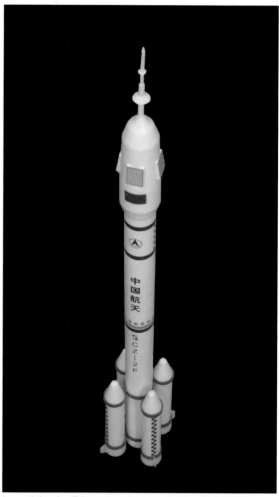

Long March 2F launch vehicle, used for Shenzhou missions   Morris Jones

have been launched by the Long March 2F launch vehicle, which is based on one of China's large satellite launch systems. Now, however, China is preparing to introduce a more powerful launch vehicle for future missions. The Long March 2F/H will resemble the Long March 2F,

Leaked image of Vehicle Assembly Building at Jiuquan
Source unknown, via Mark Wade, Encyclopedia Astronautica

Leaked image of Long March 2F launch vehicle with gantry
Source Unknown, via Mark Wade, Encyclopedia Astronautica

but will use different engines and different fuels, which will give it more lifting capacity. This will potentially allow future Shenzhou missions to fly to higher orbits, or to carry more equipment.

The Shenzhou spacecraft is a capsule-style vehicle, with three main sections. A cylindrical instrument module at its rear houses rocket engines, fuel tanks, batteries and other supplies for the mission. It also sports two large solar panels for electricity. Sitting atop this is the descent module, a bell-shaped module that holds the crew during launch and re-entry. It

is the only part of the spaceship that returns to Earth intact. This, in turn, is connected to the orbital module, a cylindrical cabin that gives the crew extra living space when they are in orbit, and also carries experimental equipment and supplies. The orbital module also carries a small set of solar panels on some missions and its own rocket thrusters. The overall design of the Shenzhou spacecraft is strongly reminiscent of the Soviet Union's Soyuz spacecraft. China has bought Russian technology to help develop Shenzhou, but stresses that the vehicle is largely built with indigenous technology.

Tiangong Space Laboratory

Soon after the Shenzhou 7 mission in 2008, China revealed plans for its next steps in human spaceflight. A small

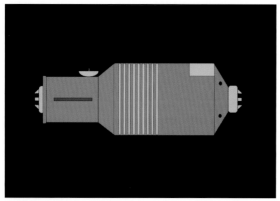

Diagram of Chinese Tiangong space laboratory
Morris Jones

'space laboratory' is to be launched in 2010 or 2011. To be known as Tiangong, it would be roughly the same size and weight as a Shenzhou spacecraft. Tiangong resembles two short cylinders joined together, with solar panels, and two docking ports. China is understood to have bought the rights to use the Russian-developed APAS docking system for its Tiangong and Shenzhou spacecraft.

Tiangong-1 will be launched by a modified version of the Long March 2F, called Long March 2F/G. This is believed to be mostly similar to the Long March 2F previously used for

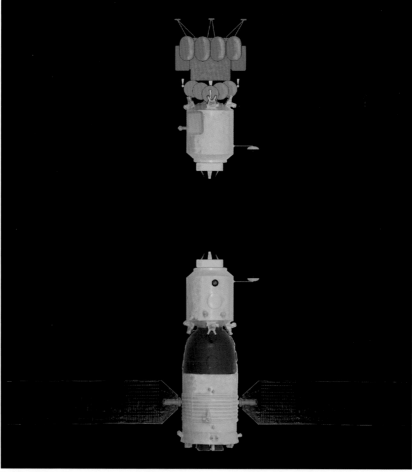

Long March 2F with modified fins and payload fairing, for carrying lunar lander to Earth orbit   Morris Jones

Undocking of a hypothetical Chinese lunar module from Lunar Shenzhou
Morris Jones

Shenzhou missions. It will have slightly longer rocket stages, but use the same engines and fuels as the Long March 2F, in contrast to the new Long March 2F/H rocket that will be used for future Shenzhou launches. One principal change for the Long March 2F/G is a larger payload shroud to accommodate the Tiangong Space Laboratory.

Soon after the launch of Tiangong-1, China plans to launch an unmanned Shenzhou spacecraft, Shenzhou 8, to rendezvous and dock with it. This will give China its first test of joining two spacecraft together in orbit. Later, another unmanned Shenzhou spacecraft, Shenzhou 9, will be launched to Tiangong-1. It is expected that Shenzhou 9 will be filled with cargo and supplies in the areas normally occupied by the crew. It is not clear how long Shenzhou 8 or Shenzhou 9 will remain docked to Tiangong-1, or which one will leave the laboratory first, but one of them will need to depart before the next mission flies to Tiangong-1, in order to leave a docking port free. While the unmanned Shenzhou spacecraft are docked to the laboratory, one of them will probably boost the laboratory's orbit by firing its own rocket motors.

The next mission will be Shenzhou 10, carrying a crew of three astronauts. They will dock with the laboratory and enter it. China has given no details on what the astronauts will do or how long they will stay, but analysts suggest they will probably remain on board the space laboratory for about two weeks. The astronauts will probably unload food and other consumables from one of the unmanned Shenzhou spacecraft docked to the station.

China has announced plans for two more space laboratories, dubbed Tiangong-2 and Tiangong-3, to be launched before 2015, and presumably very similar to Tiangong-1. China will probably make incremental improvements to each station, as it has done with successive launches of its Shenzhou spacecraft.

It is not clear how many crews will visit the space laboratories, but Tiangong-2 and Tiangong-3 are expected to host more than one manned expedition. China will probably launch more unmanned Shenzhou spacecraft to these laboratories, to serve as cargo carriers and also as backup spacecraft. Astronauts on board a Tiangong laboratory could use another Shenzhou to return to Earth if their main spacecraft experiences problems, and the unmanned Shenzhou spacecraft could be used to return experiments to Earth.

Chinese Space Station

China is calling its Tiangong spacecraft a 'space laboratory' because of its small size and the presumably short duration of crew stays. The title 'space station', implying a larger and more permanent outpost in space, has been applied to the nation's next project, currently slated for launch around 2020 and so far unnamed, to be launched using its Long March 5 vehicles.

The space station module would weigh roughly 18 tonnes, a vast increase on the roughly 8 tonnes of Tiangong. The size and interior volume would also be substantially larger. Chinese artwork suggests that the new space station module will feature some of the same engineering elements as Tiangong, and could resemble a 'stretched' version. Statements from senior officials suggest that the first Chinese space station will be constructed of three of these modules. Each will probably feature different equipment, and possibly have a slightly different design. One would probably house the crew, featuring sleeping areas, a bathroom and food preparation facilities. The other two modules could contain experiments and equipment. Chinese artwork suggests that the modules would be arranged in a T-shape, joined together at a roughly spherical docking hub. All modules would carry solar panels for power.

Crews would be launched to this space station using Shenzhou spacecraft. It seems logical to assume that there will be three astronauts on board each expedition. Other spacecraft, probably unmanned Shenzhou vehicles, will carry supplies to the station.

Astronauts on board the space station will probably stay there for several weeks or months, as China will probably want to gain experience in long-duration spaceflight.

China's next sequence of missions, along with the spacewalking experience it has already gained, will provide it with many of the capabilities required for sending astronauts beyond Earth orbit. The docking of spacecraft, transfer of crews between spacecraft, and long-duration flight were all practised by Gemini and Apollo astronauts as preparation for Moon landings.

Chinese Astronauts to the Moon

China was coy about discussing plans for sending astronauts to the Moon for many years. Reports of plans for such missions were sometimes even denied by officials. But some indicators were too obvious to ignore. The logo of the China Lunar Exploration Program (CLEP), which began operations with the Chang'e-1 mission, actually features astronauts' footprints in its centre.

After the flight of Shenzhou 7 in 2008, officials began to state openly that landing astronauts on the Moon was a long-term goal of their space program. The success of this mission had apparently given them the confidence to speak out. It also suggested that the Chinese Government had given its approval for such a venture.

No specific timetable for flying astronauts to the Moon has been released. It's possible that China has not developed any firm deadlines, but will simply accomplish various goals as technology and scheduling permit.

Will such plans be accomplished? It's difficult for anyone to predict at this stage. China has said almost nothing about its technology for carrying out these goals, but it's possible to construct a plausible set of missions, based on the current direction of the country's space program. The Shenzhou spacecraft, developed to carry astronauts into Earth orbit, could easily be used to send astronauts to the Moon.

A Chinese Circumlunar Mission

China's ultimate goal is to land astronauts on the Moon and return them to Earth. But it seems probable that they will attempt to launch astronauts to the Moon without landing before this happens. NASA launched two manned missions to the Moon without landing (Apollo 8 and Apollo 10) before the first landing was carried out by Apollo 11. The Soviet Union had plans for a similar mission, which was never actually attempted with a human crew.

As with the robot probes, China's manned lunar exploration plans are likely to be supported by the Long March 5 rockets, which would provide the power to launch heavy spacecraft into deep space. But delays in the development of these rockets, or concerns over their safety for supporting humans as passengers, could affect their usefulness in the short term. In fact, it would be entirely feasible for China to send astronauts to the Moon without the Long March 5 rockets. It would simply require the creative use of some existing technology.

China's human spaceflight program has been heavily influenced by Russian technology. The Soviet Union had plans for a circumlunar mission which would carry a modified Soyuz spacecraft around the far side of the Moon, then return it to Earth.

The Zond spacecraft were flown on free-return trajectories that used the Moon's gravity to slingshot the probes back to Earth after they had passed around the far side of the Moon. Zond demonstrated the feasibility of this technique, even though it only flew tests with animal passengers.

Shenzhou (which has the same module design as Soyuz) could be modified into a circumlunar spacecraft, similar to Zond. It would simply require the deletion of the large orbital module at its front which gives the crew extra room. Removing this would save a lot of weight. Other systems on board would need to be re-installed to compensate for the loss of the orbital module (such as relocating the toilet), but a new, reduced-mass spacecraft could be created.

A reduced Shenzhou would not be capable of supporting a three-man crew, and it seems more realistic to fly such a mission with a single passenger, as was originally planned for Zond.

A Space Tugboat

Simply launching a modified Shenzhou into space on a Long March 2F/H rocket would not be sufficient for a lunar flight. The Long March 2F/H does not have the power to send even a reduced Shenzhou to the Moon. But a second rocket could launch a 'space tugboat' into Earth orbit to do the job—a rocket stage that would dock with the Shenzhou in Earth orbit, then fire its engine to carry the spacecraft out to the Moon. Soon afterwards, the Shenzhou would undock from

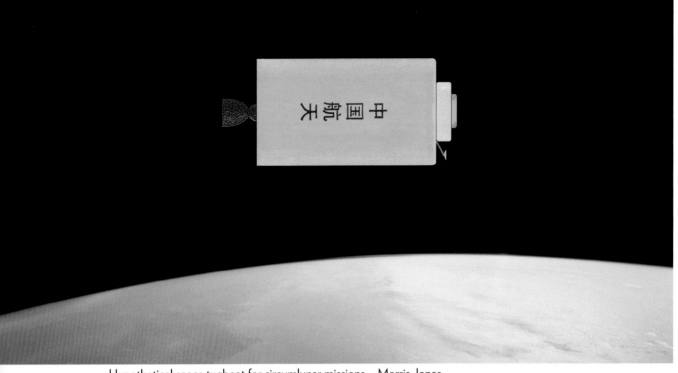

Hypothetical space tugboat for circumlunar missions   Morris Jones

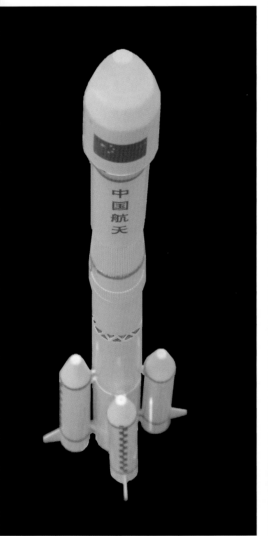

Long March 3B launch vehicle: A potential space tugboat launcher   Morris Jones

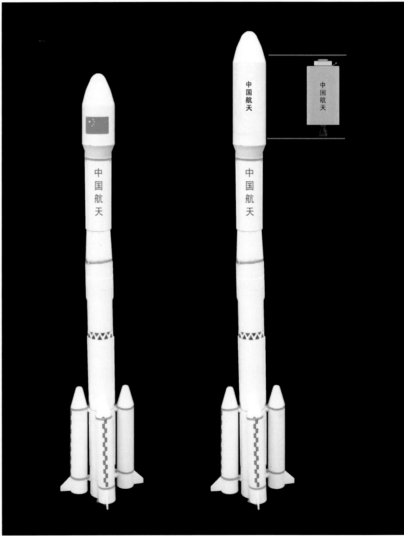

Long March 3B with conventional payload fairing and stretched fairing for space tugboat   Morris Jones

THE NEW MOON RACE

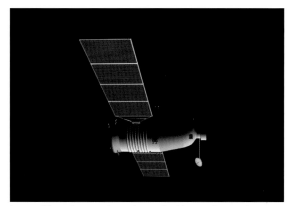

Lunar Shenzhou with tugboat docking collar replacing the Orbital Module   AGI/Morris Jones modified

the rocket stage as it left the Earth. The size and fuel requirements of the 'tugboat' rocket stage would depend on the final weight of the spacecraft. Some designs could use conventional propellants such as hydrazine and nitrogen tetroxide, while others could be fuelled with liquid hydrogen and liquid oxygen. Such a rocket stage could be launched by a modified version of the Long March 2F/H or a Long March 3B, which has a longer design heritage.

Flight to the Moon

The lunar Shenzhou would probably take three days to fly to the Moon. It would spin as it flew to even out the thermal loads on the spacecraft, with no side being 'baked' in the Sun for too long. This is technically known as passive thermal control, but was informally called 'barbecue mode' on Apollo missions.

The single crewmember would gradually see the Moon grow larger. Small burns of rocket thrusters would be made at some points to stay on course.

The hours before the closest approach to the Moon would

Fully equipped lunar Shenzhou over the far side of the Moon   AGI/NASA/Morris Jones modified

see the astronaut frantically busy with navigation, photography and broadcasts to Earth. Communications would be cut off when the spacecraft passed behind the Moon. When the 'communications blackout' ended, the Shenzhou would be rounding the Moon for the return to Earth. Another three days would pass as the spacecraft came home. Then the descent module would detach, and the spacecraft would re-enter the atmosphere, landing like a conventional Shenzhou mission.

More Advanced Missions

The mission described above represents the easiest and most basic way that China could send an astronaut to the Moon. But more sophisticated missions could be attempted.

The use of a large booster stage launched by a Long March 5 vehicle

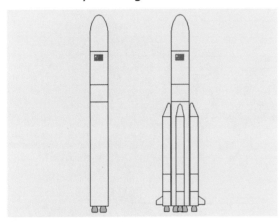

Long March 5 heavy-lift launch vehicle   Morris Jones

would permit the flight of an entire Shenzhou spacecraft on a circumlunar mission. This could carry more crew and more instruments to produce scientific observations of the Moon.

China could even elect to use a booster stage to decelerate Shenzhou upon arrival at the Moon, placing it in orbit. This was the mission profile used by Apollo 8. Orbiting the Moon would allow observations over an extended period. If only one or two crewmembers were flown, the Shenzhou's orbital module could be left behind in lunar orbit to make automatic observations, while the rest of the spacecraft returned to Earth.

Chinese Lunar Landing

The ultimate goal of China's lunar exploration is to send astronauts to the surface and return them to Earth, the most challenging task so far attempted in human spaceflight. It's worth noting that more than 360 people have flown in space, but only twelve have walked on the Moon. China is unlikely to be ready for a lunar landing mission before 2024.

A Chinese lunar landing mission could be accomplished in several different ways, but it seems reasonable to assume that they will all involve the use of Shenzhou spacecraft and Long March 5 rockets. The Long March 5 is not powerful enough to launch all of the components for a manned lunar landing with a single launch. Some form of rendezvous in Earth orbit of spacecraft components could be envisaged. Separate spacecraft to be used in the mission could also be sent on independent trajectories to the Moon, then stage a rendezvous in lunar orbit. Smaller rockets, like the Long March 3B or modified versions of the Long March 2F, could be used to carry some components to Earth orbit, where they would join with other spacecraft and rocket stages for the journey to the Moon.

The crew for a lunar landing mission would probably fly to the Moon on board a Shenzhou. A separate lunar lander would carry one or two astronauts to the surface. One astronaut would remain in lunar orbit aboard Shenzhou while his colleagues walked on the Moon. This scenario is similar to the way Apollo missions were conducted.

What would a Chinese lunar lander look like? No plans or drawings for such a vehicle have been revealed, but it is possible that the design will be influenced by China's first attempts

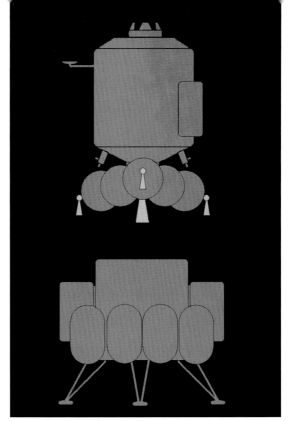

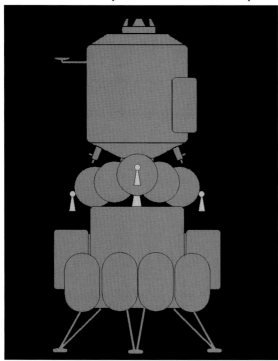

Chinese lunar lander in landing configuration
Morris Jones

Chinese Lunar Lander in early ascent phase from Moon
Morris Jones

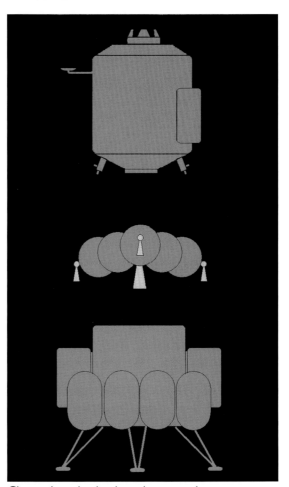

at developing robot lunar landers. It would probably have three or four landing legs, with a collection of rocket thrusters at its base. This would not be identical to the landers proposed for the rover and sample-return missions, but probably resemble a scaled-up version of the lander. Extra fuel tanks would be added to compensate for the added landing mass.

A cabin on top of this lander platform would house the crew, and be used to lift the crew off the surface to re-join with Shenzhou. This cabin could resemble the orbital module currently

Chinese lunar lander discards its propulsion stage during ascent.   Morris Jones

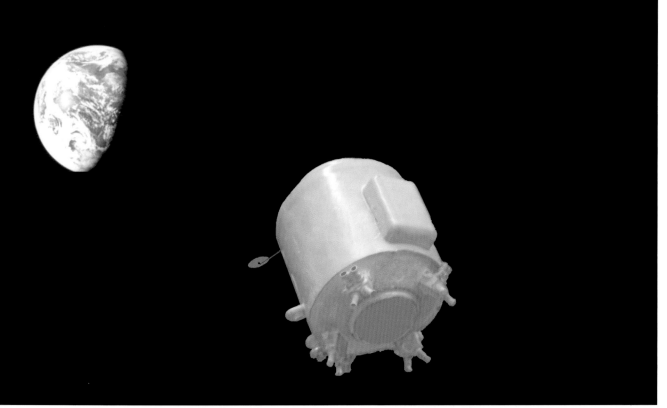

Hypothetical ascent of a Chinese lunar lander crew cabin from the Moon   Morris Jones

used on Shenzhou.

It's worth exploring the design of the Shenzhou orbital module in detail. Unlike the orbital module on the Russian Soyuz spacecraft, the Shenzhou orbital module can be flown as an independent spacecraft. On the first six Shenzhou missions (including the first two manned missions), the module carried its own set of solar panels and rocket thrusters. Shenzhou orbital modules have been left in orbit long after the rest of the spacecraft has re-entered, and flown independent missions lasting roughly six months. It's as if China is testing the ability to fly the orbital module as a new sort of vehicle. One potential application would be its use as an independent spacecraft on a lunar mission.

China has developed spacesuits for conducting spacewalks in Earth orbit, and demonstrated one on the spacewalk from Shenzhou 7 in 2008.

Before the mission flew, it was revealed that the Chinese extravehicular spacesuits are generally based on the

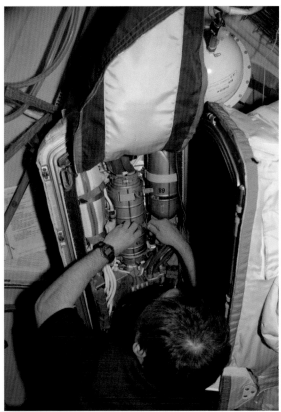

Life support system of Russian Orlan spacesuit, similar to Chinese 'Feitian' suit.   NASA

THE NEW MOON RACE

Russian Orlan suits, used for spacewalks from the International Space Station. In fact, one of the spacesuits worn on the Shenzhou 7 mission was an Orlan suit imported from Russia. Only one of the Chinese astronauts exposed to vacuum on Shenzhou 7 wore the locally produced version, known as Feitian. The Feitian suit resembles the Orlan suit, but has a modified helmet structure and instrumentation panels.

China could elect to use a modified version of its Feitian suit for astronauts who land on the Moon, the addition of special overshoes allowing the astronauts to walk on the rough terrain. The illustration on this page is a modified image, based on Russian and Chinese hardware, suggesting how such a suit might look.

It's possible that a Chinese lunar mission would land two astronauts on the surface of the Moon. The orbital module has enough room to support two spacesuits and their occupants, as Shenzhou 7 demonstrated. The astronauts would presumably collect

Chinese astronaut descends to the lunar surface   NASA/ Morris Jones

rock samples and plant the flag of China, similar to the way the Apollo astronauts worked on the Moon.

At the end of the surface phase of the mission, a small rocket stage, similar to the one used on the return stage of the proposed Chinese sample-return mission, would propel the crew cabin during its ascent. This would then

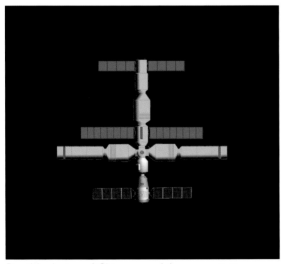

Possible design of Chinese modular space station, launched by Long March 5 rockets   AGI/Morris Jones modified

Russian-designed APAS docking system, believed to be in use on Shenzhou   NASA

separate, allowing the cabin to fly to a rendezvous with Shenzhou in lunar orbit.

After docking with Shenzhou, the Chinese moonwalkers would transfer back to the spacecraft, and the cabin of the lunar lander would then be discarded. Shenzhou would leave lunar orbit and return to Earth.

A Chinese Saturn 5?

The Long March 5 series of rockets currently in development would allow China to mount an entire manned lunar program, ranging from circumlunar flybys to landings. It would require multiple launches of these rockets to assemble lunar spacecraft complexes in Earth orbit, or launch them independently to the Moon for rendezvous in lunar orbit.

This strategy of multiple launches and rendezvous in Earth orbit was considered for the American Apollo program, but the United States quickly resolved to develop the Saturn 5 booster, a mammoth rocket that could loft all the spacecraft for a lunar landing in a single launch.

China's long-term plans for booster development beyond Long March 5 are open to question, both outside and inside the country's borders. But tentative plans are being drawn for an even more powerful vehicle, comparable in power to the Saturn 5 rocket.

This vehicle, which does not yet seem to have a precise name, would represent a huge increase in power and lifting capacity over the Long

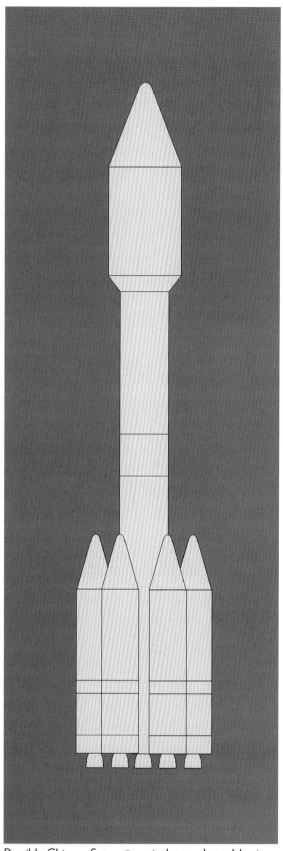

Possible Chinese Saturn 5 equivalent rocket   Morris Jones

THE NEW MOON RACE

March 5 boosters. A lifting capacity of roughly 100 tonnes to low Earth orbit is envisaged, along with the ability to launch 50 tonnes on a translunar trajectory. This exceeds the lunar payload capacity of a Saturn 5.

The development of the Saturn 5 equivalent would potentially allow China to launch Apollo-style missions to the Moon. A single rocket would send a Shenzhou spacecraft, lunar lander and interorbital transfer stages to the Moon.

Provisional diagrams of this launch vehicle have been released. The rocket would feature a cluster of six large liquid-fuelled booster rockets clustered around its first stage. A large payload fairing would give ample space for lunar spacecraft.

It is not clear when, or if, this impressive rocket will be introduced. It could possibly appear after 2020 and support lunar missions from 2024 onwards. Its development will be influenced by China's overall success with the Long March 5 rockets, and its progress with high-powered engines.

A vehicle in the class of a Saturn 5 booster would be hugely expensive to develop, one reason why other space agencies have been reluctant to introduce launch vehicles of this size. China will need to decide if the plans for using such a vehicle, or any advantages gained from it, can offset the required investment.

Apart from supporting manned lunar missions, the Saturn 5 equivalent could be used to launch large space station modules into Earth orbit, or send heavy robot probes to the planets.

Chinese Lunar Base

If China elects to embark on a substantial manned lunar program, a lunar base might be constructed. In theory, crew modules similar to those used on the Tiangong space laboratories could be adapted for this task. The modules are not very large, and would not be difficult to land. They could then be joined to form a larger volume for the crew. A small lunar base would allow astronauts to stay on the Moon for extended periods. The logistics of resupply would be cumbersome, however, and some consumables, particularly water, would need to be recycled. Toilet facilities that recycled much of the water used were introduced on the Shenzhou 7 mission. Presumably, China would use such devices on its space laboratories and its larger space station. China would probably not attempt to build a lunar base until more than one manned mission had touched down on the Moon.

As an interim step, China could elect to place a Tiangong module in lunar orbit, where it could support a crew who would fly on a separate Shenzhou flight. A Tiangong module in lunar orbit could possibly be incorporated into a mission architecture for landing astronauts on the Moon. It could serve as a halfway station for astronauts travelling between lunar orbit and the lunar surface.

Racing America

While the United States and China openly discuss their plans for lunar exploration, an obvious question must be raised. Who will send the next astronauts to the Moon? More importantly, who will land there next?

This question seems to be quietly circulating among spaceflight analysts and government officials, but it is not regularly debated in public. The issue is politically and strategically sensitive, especially in the United States, where concerns over rising Chinese economic and military strength have haunted international relations for years. Spaceflight adds another dimension to a major area of analysis. Some Americans feel that the spectre of Chinese rivalry could provide a boost to American spaceflight, encouraging the government to invest in lunar missions rather than lose to a rival state. Others feel that talk of growing Chinese capabilities is damaging to American morale.

It is difficult to speculate realistically on this subject. The timeframe is long, and well-laid plans can be easily disrupted. Political, economic and social conditions could easily upset the spaceflight plans of any nation. The United States has experienced major delays and readjustments in its own spaceflight plans over the past decade, despite the country's relatively solid economic and political stability. Political analysts generally agree that China will face its own share of political, social and economic challenges in the years ahead. Both nations are experiencing repercussions from the global financial crisis of 2008, and budget constraints could have a major influence on government support for spaceflight. However, China's authoritarian political system gives it the power to approve projects that might not enjoy large levels of popular support. If the Chinese Government wants to send astronauts to the Moon, it can muster the resources to do it, regardless of opinion polls. Feats in space exploration could be seen as one way of cementing the power of China's Communist Party in the face of a turbulent social environment.

Thus, while the matter of a second 'moon race' is a highly pressing question, it is also a very open question.

15 Russia and the Moon

The future of Russian exploration of the Moon is difficult to foresee. Plans for a new lunar program have been drawn up, but they are tempered by funding problems and political changes. Not even the Russians themselves can be totally sure of their long-term future in lunar exploration. But Russia, as a part of the now-defunct Soviet Union, has a proud if somewhat controversial heritage in flying to the Moon.

The 1960s Manned Lunar Program

The Soviet Union had drawn up plans for its own manned lunar landing in the 1960s, and a huge rocket called N-1, comparable in size to the American Saturn 5 moon rocket, was developed. This would have been used to launch two cosmonauts on board a modified Soyuz spacecraft. After arriving at the Moon, one cosmonaut would have entered a small lunar module and descended to the surface. At the end of the moonwalk, he would have returned to the module and blasted off, to rejoin his colleague on board the Soyuz in lunar orbit.

By the late 1960s, it was obvious that this plan was not going to beat Apollo to the Moon, for tests of the N-1 rocket all ended in failure. The success of the Apollo program in sending American astronauts to the Moon robbed the Soviets of the victory they had hoped to achieve. The

program was terminated in the early 1970s, and development of the N-1 rocket was also suspended. Denial of the program's existence was standard within the Soviet Union for years after its termination.

The Zond Program

A parallel (and also rival) Soviet lunar program was the Zond program. Zond, however, did not envisage landing cosmonauts on the Moon. The goal was simply to fly a single cosmonaut around the far side of the Moon, and return him to Earth.

The Zond spacecraft was a modified version of the Soyuz spacecraft, with one of the two pressurised crew modules deleted to save weight. Plans called for Zond to be launched to the Moon by a large Proton rocket, more powerful than the system used to launch Soyuz into Earth orbit.

The apparent success of early Zond test missions without cosmonauts alarmed managers at NASA, for it seemed that the Soviets had rapidly developed the capability to send a cosmonaut to the Moon. This was one reason why the Apollo 8 mission was switched from its original goal of testing the lunar module in Earth orbit to flying directly to the Moon in 1968.

In practice, the Zond program suffered from technical problems that made it unsafe for cosmonauts. Even today, the Proton rocket that was used in the program suffers from occasional launch failures. Zond never carried a cosmonaut, and the program was terminated soon after the success of Apollo 8.

Robot Lunar Probes

Russia launched an extensive series of robot probes to the Moon in the 1960s and 1970s, gradually growing in sophistication. Russia's greatest achievements in this period were the landing of two Lunokhod rovers on the Moon, the first moving vehicles to operate on the surface of another world. Each was roughly the size of a small car, and was steered remotely via radio commands from Earth. Russia also retrieved small amounts of lunar soil from its Luna robot sample-return missions. After 1976, when the last of the Luna missions flew, Russian lunar exploration entered a period of dormancy that lasted for more than 30 years.

Instruments and Rockets

The Russian Luna-Glob spacecraft, planned as an orbiter and penetrator mission for 2012, was outlined in Chapter 11. International attention on this scientifically useful mission is strong. Russia's plans for more advanced landers and rovers were also mentioned in that chapter.

Russia is supplying a rover and possibly the landing platform for the Indian Chandrayaan-2 mission, to be flown around 2011, as mentioned in Chapter 10. Little information on the rover has been published or determined

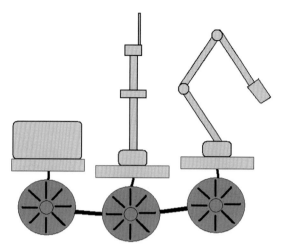

Possible Russian Moon rover design   Morris Jones

LEND instrument from Lunar Reconnaissance Orbiter   NASA

at the time of writing. It is possible that there could be similarities in the hardware designed for Chandrayaan-2 and Luna-Glob 2.

Russia is also integrating with international lunar exploration, and has provided an instrument for the Lunar Reconnaissance Orbiter, a recent US lunar probe. The lunar exploration neutron detector (LEND) instrument is designed to detect water-ice deposits at the poles and help map their distribution.

Soyuz-Fregat upper stages in vehicle assembly shop   ESA

It is possible that some nations may elect to use Russian rockets as launch vehicles for their own lunar probes in the future. The European Space Agency has already used Russian Soyuz-Fregat rockets to launch probes to Mars and Venus. This rocket is based on the classic Russian vehicle used to launch Soyuz spacecraft, but adds an additional small rocket stage known as Fregat inside the rocket's large payload fairing.

The European MoonNext mission is slated to launch on a Soyuz rocket, and other European probes could also ride this vehicle.

Russia is also preparing to introduce a new type of rocket called Angara. This is a modular rocket system, allowing the configuration of rocket stages and boosters to be changed for different sizes of payload. Angara, which should begin flying by 2011, could be used to support future lunar missions.

Russia is also preparing to launch rockets from the European Space Agency's launch site at Kourou in

Soyuz-Fregat rocket cutaway   Starsem

Soyuz-Fregat launch   Starsem-S.Corvaja-ESA

French Guiana, a site that permits launch trajectories not possible from existing launch sites in Russia and Kazakhstan. Russia is also developing a new launch site inside Russian territory

that will help reduce its dependence on Kazakhstan.

Russian Lunar Tourism

In 2001, Russia launched a private 'space tourist' into orbit. Dennis Tito, an American businessman, paid a reported US$20 million for a flight to the International Space Station on board a Soyuz spacecraft. The flight was brokered by Space Adventures, a US company that has gained the rights to market seats on Russian spacecraft. Russia has since flown other space tourists on similar missions.

In 2005, Space Adventures announced plans for an even more ambitious tourist flight. Customers could fly all the way to the Moon on board a Soyuz spacecraft. The price—a cool US$100 million per seat.

Soyuz spacecraft simulator with private space explorer Anousheh Ansari   Space Adventures

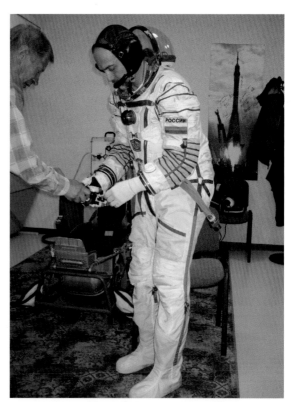

Private space explorer Richard Garriott in Russian Sokol in-flight suit   Space Adventures

THE NEW MOON RACE

International Space Station (ISS)
Staged Lunar Mission Profile

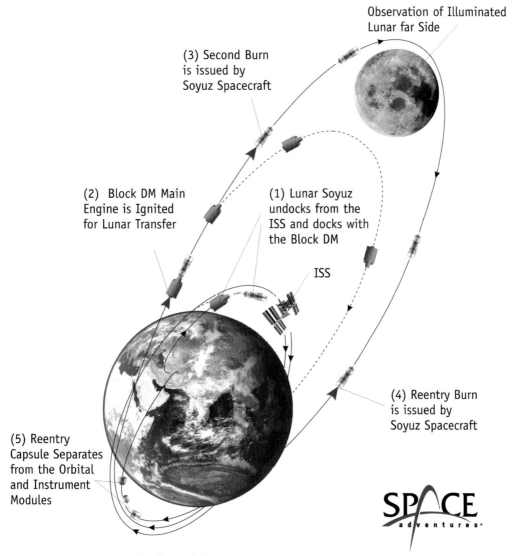

Observation of Illuminated
Lunar far Side

(3) Second Burn
is issued by
Soyuz Spacecraft

(2) Block DM Main
Engine is Ignited
for Lunar Transfer

(1) Lunar Soyuz
undocks from the
ISS and docks with
the Block DM

ISS

(4) Reentry Burn
is issued by
Soyuz Spacecraft

(5) Reentry
Capsule Separates
from the Orbital
and Instrument
Modules

SPACE
adventures

Lunar tourism mission proposal   Space Adventures

With three seats on the spacecraft, two tourists would be carried in the one mission, and accompanied by a Russian cosmonaut who would pilot the spacecraft. Alternatively, a very well-heeled space tourist who wanted more room could book both seats.

Russia's creation of space tourism to the Moon is historically interesting. No Soviet or Russian cosmonaut has ever gone there, but plans for sending spacecraft to the Moon have circulated for decades. The aborted Zond

program is the simplest example. Russia is returning to its original goals, with the help of foreign capital to support the heavy cost of such a mission.

But the proposed new tourism mission is better than Zond. A complete Soyuz spacecraft would be launched into Earth orbit by a conventional Soyuz launch vehicle. The Soyuz will then probably dock at the International Space Station, where the tourist will enjoy a holiday in Earth orbit for roughly ten days. At the end of this

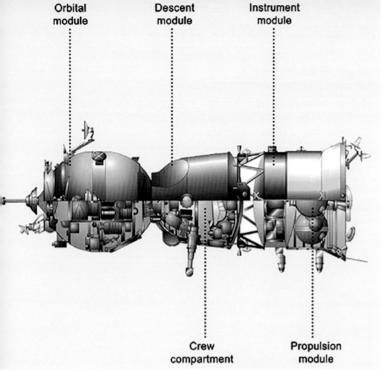

Orbital module   Descent module   Instrument module

Crew compartment   Propulsion module

Soyuz spacecraft modules   ESA

Soyuz rocket on launchpad   NASA/JSC

Soyuz rocket in assembly   NASA/JSC

first phase of the mission, the Soyuz would undock for another rendezvous. During launch, landing and docking, the Soyuz crew would wear lightweight Russian-developed Sokol in-flight spacesuits that would protect them in the event of a loss of cabin pressure.

The Soyuz would dock with a special rocket booster stage (known as a Block DM), launched by another rocket, probably a Ukrainian-built Zenit. The booster would propel Soyuz out of Earth orbit toward the Moon, on a journey lasting roughly three days. Once the booster had finished firing, it would be discarded. Soyuz would rotate slowly as it cruised to the Moon, to spread the heating of the sun evenly across its surface. The tourist would see the Earth's horizon grow more curved until the whole Earth was finally visible as a blue ball. This whole view of the Earth cannot be seen from Earth orbit. The Moon would gradually grow closer and larger.

The Soyuz would travel around the far side of the Moon, using the Moon's gravity to slingshot it back to Earth. There would be no Moon landing. Roughly three days after reaching the Moon, Soyuz would parachute to Earth. A flight like this is officially known as a circumlunar mission.

At the time of writing, it is unclear when, or if, such a grand expedition will take place. Russia would probably need to fly at least one test mission with professional cosmonauts on board before any paying passengers could be accepted. This would require considerable investment. A

Engines of Soyuz rocket   NASA/Bill Ingalls

Inspection of Soyuz fairing   NASA/JSC

Soyuz rocket is carried to launchpad by train   NASA/JSC

Soyuz spacecraft launch   NASA

Soyuz rocket above flame trench of launchpad   NASA/Bill Ingalls

representative of Space Adventures has claimed that lunar missions could be feasible after 2012.

There is also the question of who would qualify as a potential lunar tourist. Selecting candidates for ordinary Soyuz tourist flights to Earth orbit has been difficult enough, with the participants required to undertake extensive training, pass stringent

Soyuz spacecraft prepares for docking   NASA/JSC

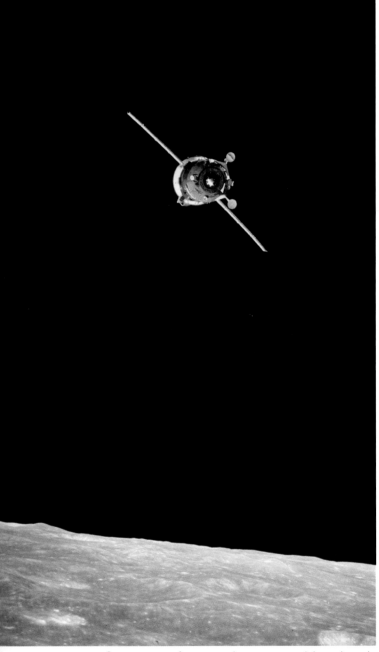

Soyuz spacecraft on circumlunar mission   Morris Jones/ NASA

medical and technical exams, and supply seven-figure sums of cash. The constraints on prospective lunar tourists would be even more severe, including the enormous financial burdens.

Is Russia prepared to fly a circumlunar mission without the guarantee of foreign currency? Is the prospect of lunar tourism the fulcrum of the program, or merely an additional incentive? The answers are unclear.

The Euro-Russian Partnership

In 2008, Russia and the European Space Agency announced a deal to develop a new manned spacecraft that would replace the venerable Soyuz that has flown since 1967. Soyuz has undergone several upgrades to its propulsion, life-support and computer systems over the years, but the overall modular design has not changed.

Russia had been studying replacements for Soyuz for several years, but plans for new spacecraft had previously failed to generate financial and political support. The partnership with ESA would have allowed Russia to defray the large cost of developing a new spacecraft. ESA had also wanted to develop a manned spacecraft for decades, but its plans had also failed to generate sufficient funding.

The proposed new spacecraft was a capsule-style vehicle with a blunt, conical crew module and a cylindrical instrument module behind it. Resemblances to the Apollo spacecraft and the new Orion spacecraft were obvious. Russia was slated to build the crew capsule, while ESA would develop the service module. The capsule was

Soyuz spacecraft descends   NASA/JSC

Earthrise from the Moon   NASA

Soyuz spacecraft landing in Kazakhstan   NASA/JSC

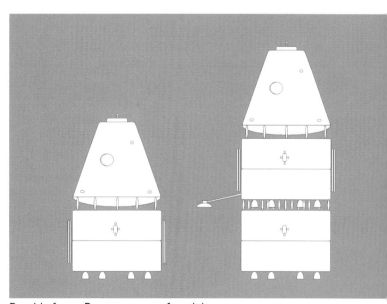

Possible future Russian spacecraft, with lunar
versions   Morris Jones

designed to carry a maximum crew of six.

Discussions of plans for the joint spacecraft went lukewarm for several months, before the partnership between ESA and Russia finally dissolved in late 2008. ESA apparently decided to withdraw from the project due to disagreements over funding and contract allocation. Political tensions could also have added to the problems.

A New Russian Spacecraft

The dissolution of the partnership with the European Space Agency did not, however, destroy plans for a new Russian spacecraft. Russia holds the capability to develop a similar vehicle by itself. At the time of writing, Russia seems to be still pursuing plans for a new six-person spacecraft, with a design that would probably be similar to the craft proposed for the Euro-Russian partnership.

The final design of this vehicle has not been precisely determined. The exact timeline for its development and first flight are also open to question. Changes to the overall appearance are possible, especially with regard to the service module. The illustration on page 131 is a hypothetical depiction of a revised vehicle design.

While the first flights of this vehicle will carry Russian cosmonauts into Earth orbit, Russian officials have also spoken of flights beyond Earth, to the Moon. The vehicle could be sent on circumlunar missions with the aid of a rendezvous with a booster stage in Earth orbit. Full lunar orbital missions would require extra fuel, and one way of supplying this would be the addition of a second service module at the rear, which would handle the deceleration of the vehicle into lunar orbit. This stage could then be discarded, allowing the primary service module to handle the return to Earth. But this is all hypothetical. The illustration depicts two versions of the craft, one for Earth orbit, the other for lunar missions.

The Soyuz launch vehicle, which takes its name from the spacecraft it launches, is not powerful enough to launch this new spacecraft, and an alternative launch system will have to be used. Options include the Zenit rocket, which is built in the former Soviet republic of Ukraine, or the development of a new launch vehicle.

Russian Geopolitics
The renewed support for spaceflight in Russia seems to be connected to a resurgence in national pride and posturing as the country emerges from the chaos of the fall of the Soviet Union in 1991. Russian strategic ventures have grown more assertive in recent years, including military incursions into former Soviet states. Spaceflight is a traditional expression of Russian strength as a superpower.

Russia's turbulent political and strategic activities could also influence ventures with other nations, the dissolution of the Euro-Russian capsule project being an example.

Russia has enjoyed substantial economic growth in the twenty-first century, partially due to massive development of its oil and gas reserves. Increased revenue has apparently given the nation the confidence to propose a robust space program to emulate the feats of the Soviet era. The economic turbulence of late 2008 threatened to harm economic growth, although its long-term influence on the economy was unclear. A decrease in economic strength could seriously affect Russia's spaceflight plans, including the development of its new spacecraft and plans for lunar missions.

Extending Soyuz
In the event that Russia is unable to develop its new six-person capsule, another option could present itself. Russia could simply continue flying the Soyuz spacecraft for an extended period. Soyuz has proven to be a highly robust and dependable spacecraft, with

THE NEW MOON RACE

a long development heritage behind it, and some space enthusiasts could be reluctant to abandon a design that already works.

A slightly improved version of the latest Soyuz spacecraft, known as Soyuz TMA, is expected to begin flying in 2009 or 2010. In taking further advantage of existing infrastructure and

Soyuz TMA spacecraft   NASA

know-how for manufacturing Soyuz, Russia could avoid the costs and uncertainty of developing an entirely new spacecraft.

Earlier plans for new Soyuz variants suggested expanding the orbital module at the front of the spacecraft, which contains the docking probe and hatch. The current module is roughly spherical in shape, but a new module would probably be a short cylinder. A larger orbital module would give the crew more room, and allow more equipment to be carried. No such plan has yet been implemented, but could be re-examined if other spacecraft options prove untenable. An expanded Soyuz would be more suitable for lunar missions, as the crew will need to occupy the spacecraft for an extended period, but even if it is approved it would probably not fly before 2012. It is entirely possible that Soyuz will celebrate its 50th anniversary in 2017 as the world's longest operational spacecraft.

Russian Lunar Landings

In the present climate, it is difficult to say how or when Russian cosmonauts could land on the Moon. Russia would presumably wish to launch several manned missions to lunar orbit before such a feat was attempted, probably involving a separate lunar landing spacecraft. Realistically, no Russian manned lunar landing can be expected before 2020.

Mission Control Centre, Korolyov, Russia   NASA/JSC

16 European Manned Missions

Europe has already gained a small foothold in robot lunar exploration, and has plans for more missions in the future. But Europe is also forging the hardware that could be used for sending its own astronauts directly to the Moon on European spacecraft. No firm plans for launching astronauts to the Moon have yet been drafted or funded, but it would be entirely possible for a European manned lunar program to develop in the decades ahead.

The Booster

The European Space Agency has steadily built up its experience with its own heavy-lift rocket. The Ariane 5 had a somewhat dubious performance record in its early years, but has gradually grown more reliable. Advanced versions have boosted lift capacity. This rocket could easily serve as the principal launch system for sending European astronauts to the Moon.

Ariane 5 is a large, liquid-fuelled rocket that burns liquid hydrogen and liquid oxygen as its main propellants. Its thrust is supplemented by the addition of two large solid rocket boosters on its side. Overall, the huge liquid fuel tank and solid booster combination is slightly reminiscent of a space shuttle's external fuel tank and boosters.

Ariane 5 rocket   ESA

Ariane 5 is launched from the European Space Agency's principal launch site at Kourou in French Guiana, at a point near to the Equator on the coast of South America, giving the rocket an extra boost from the Earth's rotation. The most powerful version of the rocket stands 53 metres tall, and can place as much as 21 tonnes in low Earth orbit.

ATV in testing   ESA/ S.Corvaja

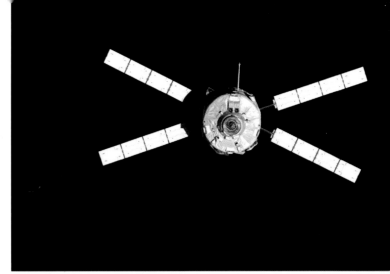

ATV Jules Verne in orbit   NASA

Ariane 5 with ATV   ESA/ D. Ducros

Propulsion system for ATV   ESA/S. Corvaja

ATV flies close to the International Space Station   NASA

ATV departs from the International Space Station   NASA

Detail of ATV docking system   NASA

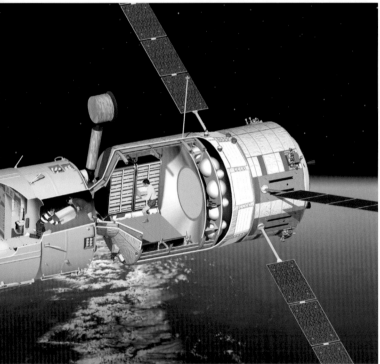

ATV docked with the International Space Station   ESA/D. Ducros

(Below) Comparison of ATV with Russian Progress cargo ship and Apollo spacecraft   ESA/ D. Ducros

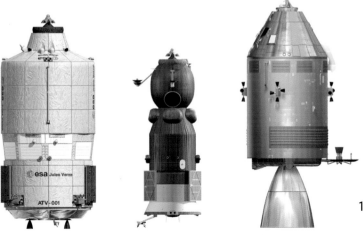

ATV   Progress   Apollo

Automated Transfer Vehicle

The Automated Transfer Vehicle (ATV) is a new European spacecraft, launched by the Ariane 5 rocket. It is designed as a giant cargo and logistics vessel for the International Space Station. The first ATV, dubbed Jules Verne (after the pioneering French science fiction writer), was launched in March 2008. It carried a huge assortment of supplies, including food, water, oxygen, fuel and equipment. The ATV also serves as a 'tugboat', firing its own rocket motors to boost the station's orbit. It is designed to remain docked to the International Space Station for roughly six months while its supplies are gradually unloaded and its large pressurised payload bay is filled with trash and used equipment. At the end of its mission, the ATV undocks from the space station, fires its rocket motors, and destructively re-enters the atmosphere. At least seven ATV missions are planned for resupplying the International Space Station.

The ATV looks like a huge cylinder with a Russian-designed docking system at its front. The docking system is identical to that of the Russian Soyuz spacecraft and the Russian Progress cargo supply spacecraft that is modelled on Soyuz. ATV has a

136

cylindrical service module at its rear, containing rocket motors, fuel tanks and solar panels. The forward section is the pressurised compartment that stores cargo.

Impressive in size, ATV is more than 10 metres long, and is 4.5 metres wide. Its cargo capacity is roughly three times that of the Russian Progress cargo spacecraft, flying since the 1970s. Its size is comparable to an American Apollo spacecraft, which to date is the largest capsule spacecraft flown.

The first flight of ATV proved so successful that its service time at the International Space Station was extended. Astronauts used the empty cargo hold for additional living space (and as a bathroom where they took sponge baths).

Early European Plans

In the 1980s, the ESA dabbled with the idea of developing a miniature winged space shuttle, dubbed Hermes. Hermes was to be launched on top of an Ariane 5 rocket and carry astronauts into space. Hermes was never built due to funding constraints, but Europe has still experimented with the elements for a manned European spacecraft.

One test flight, known as the Atmospheric Re-entry Demonstrator (ARD), saw a conical capsule that resembled a scaled-down American Apollo capsule launched into space on an Ariane 5 mission in 1998. The ARD re-entered the atmosphere, splashed down successfully, and was recovered. There were no astronauts on board. ARD showed that Europe could recover objects from space.

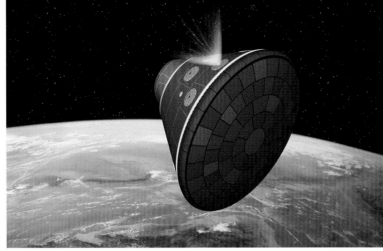
ARD re-entry demonstrator capsule   ESA/D. Ducros

ARD capsule during re-entry   ESA/D. Ducros

ARD capsule after landing   ESA/ S.Corvaja

Europe has also worked on design studies for crew rescue vehicles for the International Space Station that also resembled conical Apollo-style capsules. These designs have not produced any actual vehicles.

In 2008, Europe formed an unsuccessful, short-lived partnership with Russia to develop a new spacecraft which would also be used by Russia to replace its existing Soyuz spacecraft.

A European Spacecraft

Following the collapse of the partnership with Russia, Europe now has the option of developing a wholly European spacecraft for launching astronauts. A prototype of a conical capsule has already been exhibited. Developed by the aerospace group EADS-Astrium, the capsule was being developed in parallel to the negotiations with Russia as a fallback option. Work on the capsule was suspended when Russia formed a partnership with Europe to develop the crew capsule for the proposed new European-Russian manned spacecraft.

The EADS-Astrium capsule design shares much in common with the original Euro-Russian proposal. It is a steep cone, designed to sit atop a conical service module. The small rocket placed atop the capsule is an escape system, designed to pull the capsule away from its launch vehicle in the event of an emergency.

The photographs on this and the facing page are of a model exhibited at an air show in Berlin in 2008, which lacked much of the detail of an actual

European-designed manned capsule proposed by EADS   EADS-Astrium/Ingo Wagner/2008

Interior of European capsule proposed by EADS   EADS-Astrium/Ingo Wagner/2008

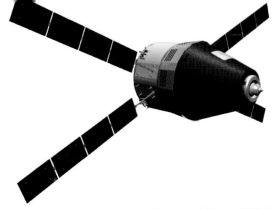

ESA illustration of Advanced Re-entry Vehicle (ARV)
ESA/D. Ducros

Heatshield of European capsule proposed by
EADS   EADS-Astrium/Ingo Wagner/2008

spacecraft. The suspension of work on the project means that some of the finer details of the spacecraft have not yet been resolved. The model's interior crew cabin, for example, is highly provisional. It remains to be seen if this EADS proposal will serve as the basis for any real European spacecraft.

The European Space Agency is also studying an evolved version of the Automated Transfer Vehicle, called the Advanced Re-entry Vehicle, or ARV. This is an ATV with a conical re-entry capsule at its front, designed to return experiments and gear from the International Space Station. The earliest versions were not expected to be suitable for humans, but European statements did not hide the fact that the ARV could lead to the development of a system for launching astronauts. Artwork published on the website of the European Space Agency openly depicts such a spacecraft sitting atop an Ariane 5 rocket, with an escape rocket system placed atop the capsule. An escape rocket system is only placed on vehicles carrying astronauts.

Will these design studies lead to the development of an actual vehicle? The global financial crisis of 2008 saw Europe's political leaders undertake a wide range of budgetary reforms, and spaceflight is not expected to escape

Advanced Re-entry Vehicle (ARV) atop Ariane 5 rocket
ESA/D. Ducros

funding cuts. Development of a re-entry capsule for either equipment or astronauts appeared to be in a state of flux at the time of writing, and it seems likely that development plans will be pushed back until the crisis has subsided, and a new round of budgetary allocations planned for European spaceflight.

At some point in the near future, Europe will almost certainly begin development of a capsule spacecraft system. It will probably resemble the prototype designs that have previously been exhibited. This will largely be driven by the need to maintain momentum in Europe's space program, and reduce European dependence on foreign spacecraft. Without such a vehicle, Europe cannot remain a first-class space power.

Europe in Orbit
Europe has been using Soyuz spacecraft to carry astronauts to the International Space Station for years.

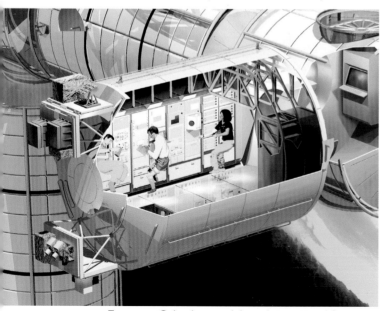

European Columbus module on International Space Station   ESA/D. Ducros

It has also constructed a laboratory module, named Columbus, which was added to the Station in 2008. Columbus was carried in the cargo bay of a space shuttle.

The introduction of a new European spacecraft would continue this trend. Europe could also elect to develop a small independent space station in Earth orbit, possibly with Russian participation, once the current International Space Station has been abandoned.

Eventually, European human space-flight could reach beyond Earth orbit.

European Lunar Spacecraft
A European lunar mission could be undertaken with the use of two Ariane 5 rocket launches to assemble a lunar complex in Earth orbit. First, an ATV-developed lunar transfer vehicle would be launched. This would closely resemble a current ATV design, but would essentially be a lunar tugboat. The pressurised cargo module found at the front of a regular ATV would be gone. The service module, which makes up roughly a third of the length of a regular ATV, would be extended. Such a vehicle would probably spend weeks, even months, in Earth orbit while it waited for the second phase of the mission. During this time, the second Ariane 5 would be prepared for launch at Kourou, and the lunar transfer vehicle would be tested with short firings of its rocket boosters.

The second Ariane 5 launch would place a European manned capsule spacecraft in orbit. Up to four crew members could be aboard.

The capsule spacecraft would rendezvous and dock with the lunar transfer vehicle, probably in a nose-to-nose docking. The lunar transfer vehicle would then fire its engines to send the complex out of Earth orbit and on its way to the Moon.

The lunar transfer vehicle would then separate, and the capsule spacecraft would begin its cruise, probably placing itself into a 'barbecue roll' to even out the heating and cooling from the Sun. The spacecraft would fly a free-return trajectory, passing over the far side of the Moon as its gravity hurled it back to Earth. As it neared home, the crew capsule would separate from its service module, and re-enter for a splashdown.

More advanced vehicles, with greater fuel loads, could even place the spacecraft in lunar orbit.

European Lunar Landing

A future European capsule could possibly be modified to land on the Moon, sending the entire crew directly to the lunar surface. Alternatively, Europe could develop a small lunar lander to carry astronauts to the surface. No precise plans for Moon landers have been drafted yet, and plans for lunar landings are unresolved. No independent European landing can be contemplated before 2020.

European Lunar Space Station

An intriguing possibility that has emerged from some European studies is the concept of a small lunar space station. This would allow astronauts to observe the Moon from orbit and conduct experiments in near-lunar

space. It could also be used as a waystation for astronauts travelling to and from the surface of the Moon.

A European lunar space station could be based on technology already developed for the International Space Station. Europe has constructed a node for docking modules on the station, with six docking ports on its cylindrical exterior. This module, known as Node 2 or Harmony, was mainly built in Italy. Modules such as this could serve as the basis for a European space station in Earth orbit or lunar orbit. The illustration at the top of page 142 envisages a hypothetical European station based on the Harmony design. Solar panels, thermal radiators and a communications antenna have been added. Docking adaptors for various types of international spacecraft could be added to the many docking ports this station would feature.

Astronauts on the surface of the Moon could use a lunar space station as a safe haven in the event of an

European Node 2 Harmony for International Space Station   NASA

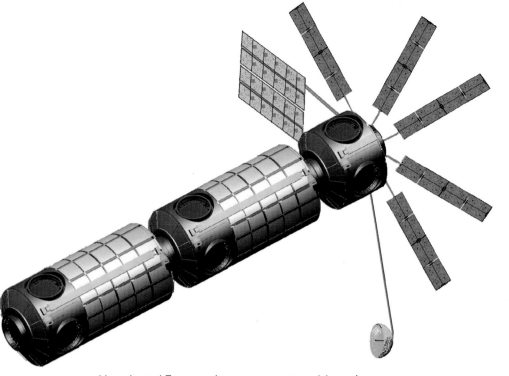

Hypothetical European lunar space station   Morris Jones

Interior of Node 2 Harmony   NASA

merged with those of other nations as part of a multi-national effort. The sheer cost of such missions could generate the need for international partnerships.

Exactly how such a partnership would be constructed remains unclear. Europe would have the options of working with nations such as China, Russia and the United States. International politics could change drastically in the future, and arrangements that have been impossible in the past could become feasible.

Harmony is prepared for launch   NASA

emergency. They could blast off from the lunar surface in their landing craft and dock with the station, where they would have access to supplies and possibly medical facilities.

Modules for this space station could be launched individually by European rockets and be joined together in Earth orbit before being transferred to the Moon. Alternatively, the modules could be flown to the Moon individually and assembled there.

International Partnerships
European plans for human lunar exploration could, in due course, be

17 Japanese and Indian Manned Missions

Japan and India host advanced space programs, and both nations have embarked on ambitious plans for lunar exploration. But will they send astronauts to the Moon? The state of space activity at present suggests that neither will participate in human lunar exploration in the near future.

Human Spaceflight in Japan

Japan has developed powerful launch vehicles, sophisticated satellites and advanced scientific capabilities in its space program. Japan has its own astronaut corps and has launched several astronauts aboard the US Space Shuttle. A Japanese television journalist also flew a privately funded mission to the now-defunct Russian Mir space station on a Soyuz spacecraft.

In 2008, the first segment of Japan's Kibo module was launched to the International Space Station by the US Space Shuttle. Later flights completed the assembly of this sophisticated laboratory. When it was completed, Kibo was actually larger than the European Columbus module on the International Space Station, which also launched in 2008. Japan has experimented with re-entry vehicles and has recovered a simple capsule from orbit.

(Right) Japanese H2B launch vehicle   JAXA

But Japan remains generally uncommitted to the deployment of a crew-carrying spacecraft. It is unclear when the nation will develop such a capability, or if it will be achieved at any stage in the next two decades.

Japan's next major project in human spaceflight is the H2 Transfer Vehicle, or HTV. This is a robotic cargo-carrying spacecraft, similar in size and

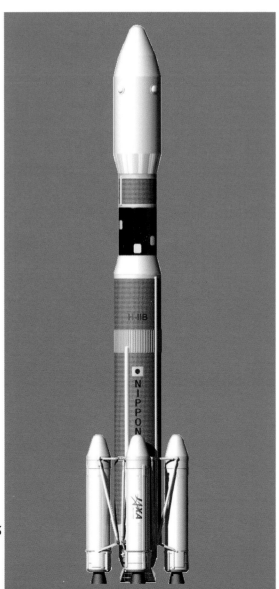

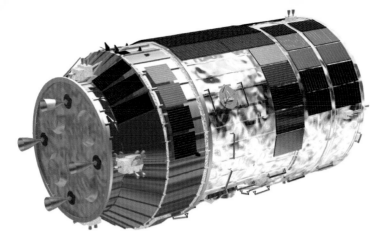

Japanese HTV cargo spacecraft   JAXA

HTV in preparation for launch   JAXA

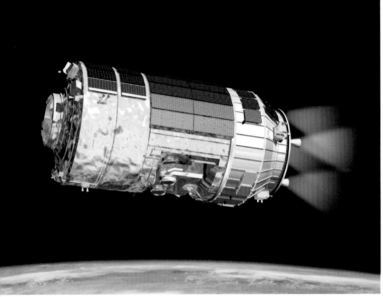

HTV boosts its orbit   JAXA

(Below) HTV separates from the final stage of its H2B launcher   JAXA

shape to the European Automated Transfer Vehicle (ATV). The HTV is a cylindrical craft, consisting of a pressurised cargo compartment and a propulsion section at its rear. It will be launched by the Japanese H2B rocket, an upgraded version of the H2A that launched the Kaguya probe

Artist's impression of H2B launch   JAXA

to the Moon. HTV has no capability for returning to Earth, and will be destroyed in the atmosphere after it has completed its mission to the International Space Station. The first of several such missions will lift off in 2009. HTV has a larger cargo capacity than the European ATV but does not have its sophisticated rendezvous and docking system. HTV vehicles will approach the International Space Station, then be guided to a dock by the station's robot arm.

HTV holds some of the elements required for a Japanese crew-carrying spacecraft. It has a propulsion and navigation system, as well as a large internal volume. But Japan does not seem to be actively researching an evolved version of HTV, unlike the way that Europe is adapting ATV technology for a future crew capsule.

In theory, Japan could cobble together the basic elements of a crew carrier from its existing technology. The HTV would serve as the propulsion and service module. A pressurised compartment for the crew could be based on technology developed for the Kibo module. Re-entry systems could also be adapted from Japan's small re-entry capsule test. But such plans are generally not discussed in even a hypothetical sense in open forums.

Recent statements from scientists suggest that Japan is interested in eventually participating in human lunar exploration. Their human lunar spaceflight will probably be conducted as part of an international project, using spacecraft and launch vehicles developed by other nations. This would continue the current Japanese trend of launching astronauts aboard foreign vehicles. Exactly how Japan would integrate its plans with the international community is unclear, as most plans for international lunar missions are vaguely defined at best. Japan will probably adopt a wait-and-see approach before endorsing or financially supporting any such venture.

Human Spaceflight in India

Like China, India is a major spacefaring nation that is not a participant in the International Space Station. It does not send astronauts to the station on foreign vehicles, and does not currently have an astronaut corps. India launched a cosmonaut to the Salyut 7 space station on a Soyuz spacecraft in 1984, but plans for later flights by Indian astronauts on the US Space Shuttle did not eventuate.

India has developed its own fleet of rockets and has launched a spacecraft to the Moon. India also staged a capsule recovery experiment from space in 2007, when a bullet-shaped spacecraft was placed in orbit and later returned to a splashdown landing in the Indian Ocean. The stage has been set for more ambitious feats in the future.

In 2008, India's space agency, ISRO, presented to the government for consideration a formal report on human spaceflight. This calls for the development of an Indian capsule spacecraft for Earth orbital missions.

India has drawn up plans to cooperate with Russia in the

development of its new human spaceflight program. An Indian cosmonaut will fly on a Russian Soyuz mission to the International Space Station in 2013. Russia will also assist India in the development of its own manned spacecraft, which Indian statements suggest will be a modified version of the Soyuz spacecraft. China had previously adapted the basic design of Soyuz for its Shenzhou manned spacecraft, and it will be interesting to see how India adapts Soyuz for its particular purposes.

The first flight of the Indian spacecraft, which does not yet have a proper name, is planned for 2015. It would be launched aboard a Geosynchronous Satellite Launch Vehicle (GSLV), the most powerful rocket currently flown by India. This rocket is substantially more powerful than the rocket used to launch the Chandrayaan-1 orbiter to the Moon.

Plans for the mission call for two astronauts to be launched aboard the vehicle and spend roughly a week in orbit.

With its human spaceflight program in its earliest stages, it seems unlikely that India can seriously consider solo manned lunar exploration for a long time. However, the growing ties between India and Russia in lunar exploration suggest that their cooperation could provide one pathway for sending Indian astronauts to the Moon.

Eventually, India could develop

Hypothetical Indian lunar landing.   Thejes

a more advanced orbital spacecraft which could later serve as the basis for lunar missions. Alternatively, a single astronaut could be sent on a circumlunar flight aboard a variation of India's first spacecraft. This would require a heavy version of the GSLV rocket. India has already proposed developing more advanced versions of this rocket in the future. Some could be powerful enough to support a modest lunar program.

A second-generation Indian capsule could be launched on a circumlunar trajectory after docking with a booster rocket in Earth orbit. It is not clear if India's first-generation capsule would have the capability to perform rendezvous and docking, but the technology could be extended in successive missions. Rivalry with other Asian powers could drive India to develop such a capability.

In due course, India could elect to participate in an international manned lunar program, assuming that financial and political considerations allowed for it.

Russian Soyuz launch   Bill Ingalls/NASA

18 Private Lunar Missions

During the 1990s, a handful of private companies announced plans for private Moon missions. These were all to be robot probes, with a variety of purposes and funding sources. Some companies planned to fly scientific instruments to the Moon and sell the data they obtained to government and scientific agencies. Other schemes included beaming back live television pictures from lunar orbit, charging people to remotely control a rover on the surface of the Moon, crashing a spacecraft filled with personal items into the Moon, or retrieving lunar rocks to sell on Earth. None of these missions was actually launched. In retrospect, this demonstrated that it's difficult to launch a mission to the Moon without government funding.

The New X Prize

A US-based private group, the X Prize Foundation, which designs and manages public competitions for the benefit of humanity in several areas of endeavour, made history in 2005 when it awarded the Ansari X Prize to the builders of the first private manned spaceship. (Anousheh Ansari, a member of the group of Iranian-American entrepreneurs who sponsored the hefty purse, flew a privately sponsored mission to the International Space Station in 2006.)

Scaled Composites, a company founded by the American aerospace engineer Burt Rutan, produced a bullet-shaped winged vehicle dubbed Space Ship One which could carry up to three people on short hops outside the atmosphere, before gliding to a runway landing. Space Ship One made three flights in its career, two of which were staged to win the US$10 million Ansari X Prize. Rutan later teamed up with British entrepreneur Sir Richard Branson, and is developing a new spacecraft to carry tourists on short sub-orbital space missions.

Despite the value of the Ansari X Prize, the money did not cover the development costs of Space Ship One. But it provided extra incentive for teams to develop private manned spacecraft. Several other companies are planning to introduce new passenger spacecraft in the future. The Ansari X Prize drew attention to the possibilities of private spaceflight, attracting interest from the media and the general public.

The concept of private lunar missions received a boost in September 2007 when the X Prize Foundation announced the Google Lunar X Prize (commonly known as the GLXP), a multimillion dollar prize for the first private group to land a robotic rover on the Moon, drive it around, and return pictures and video to Earth. A group that succeeds in landing a spacecraft on the Moon, driving a lunar rover for

Apollo 11 astronaut Buzz Aldrin at the Google Lunar X Prize launch   Aero News Network

Other upcoming private space ventures have been bankrolled by wealthy entrepreneurs looking for new challenges. The founder of the online retailer Amazon.com is sponsoring a new sub-orbital manned rocket, and the developer of the technology for Pay Pal is developing satellite launch vehicles. The advent of Google, the popular Web search engine, as the principal sponsor of the latest X Prize is a continuation of this trend.

It's hard to know which of the two X Prize challenges is the more difficult. Human spaceflight, especially in a re-useable vehicle, demands meticulous attention to safety—but navigating to the Moon, landing softly, and then performing complex robotic operations is no easy feat either.

Intermediate Goals

500 metres and transmitting a specified quantity of data back to Earth, including pictures, before the end of 2012, stands to win a prize of US$20 million. If the prize is not claimed by then, an award of $15 million will be paid to any group which accomplishes the same tasks by the end of 2014. The prize pool, which has a grand total of $30 million, includes a $5 million prize for the second team to achieve these goals and $5 million in bonus prizes for performing additional tasks on the Moon. If no team succeeds in landing a private mission to the Moon by the end of 2014, the prize offer will probably be terminated. The Google Lunar X Prize seems to be generating the same level of interest as its predecessor, which set a precedent for the operation of such a challenge.

While the world waits for a launch attempt at the Google Lunar X Prize, some groups are honing their skills by aiming for more intermediate goals. The X Prize Foundation stages an annual contest in the United States for prototype robotic lunar landers, inviting the media and the general public to watch the results. The vehicles are expected to take off, fly around and touch down safely, with large cash prizes for the winners. Armadillo Aerospace, a small US start-up company, has gained fame and notoriety for its regular appearances at these events. Armadillo has developed a strange-looking lander that mostly consists of four metal fuel tanks joined together with piping. This vehicle has repeatedly demonstrated the ability to take off, hover, and land again. It has also experienced some crashes, which are probably as entertaining to spectators as successful flights.

Is the Armadillo lander a precursor to a real lunar vehicle? Possibly. But landing on the Moon will require a design different from this bare-bones vehicle.

Going for the Prize

Soon after the announcement of the Google Lunar X Prize, several teams had registered to compete. If experience with the Ansari X Prize is any guide, most teams will not get off the ground, literally. Some have already withdrawn. A small number will probably come close to launching, and one will probably succeed in winning the prize.

Some of these teams have a lot of credentials, including prominent robotics experts and aerospace personnel. They are raising capital, and one team is based in a well-known international tax haven. But it is unclear how far each team has gone, and if they can go far enough to launch a mission.

How do you go about competing for the Google Lunar X Prize? Some of the groups that have registered are highly secretive about their plans, citing

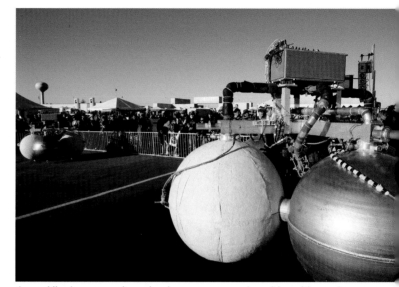

Private Moon rover explores the Moon   X Prize Foundation

Armadillo Aerospace lunar lander prototype   Aero News Network

Armadillo Aerospace lander is recovered after landing
Aero News Network

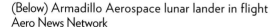
(Below) Armadillo Aerospace lunar lander in flight
Aero News Network

GLXP entry with airbag descent system   X Prize Foundation

GLXP entry with unconventional roving system X Prize Foundation

GLXP entry with conventional lander   X Prize Foundation

GLXP entry with small rover and lander   X Prize Foundation

GLXP lander descends   X Prize Foundation

GLXP entry with large lander   X Prize Foundation

confidentiality agreements and the desire to avoid helping their competitors. But we can speculate on a framework for running a private lunar mission.

The rover design will probably use a lot of existing technology. Cameras, computers, robot arms, communications systems and solar panels are easy to obtain. Certifying them for operation in the harsh conditions of the Moon would probably require some parts to be modified, but developing the rover would probably be the easiest of the three task stages of the attempt.

Although procuring a launch vehicle would be straightforward, the principal difficulty with this phase of the project would be its cost. The price of a launch vehicle capable of lofting a substantial payload to the Moon probably runs into tens of millions of dollars. For some ventures, the launch costs alone could exceed the value of the prize.

Developing a landing stage for the rover would be the trickiest part. It requires complex rocket engine technology to carefully decelerate an object to a soft landing on another world. Deploying ramps or other systems to release the rover would be needed. The lander would also need to be kept within the weight limitations of the launch vehicle. Some entries might use airbag-style descent stages, which could simplify the engineering.

A Realistic Goal?

The Ansari X Prize was claimed fairly rapidly, because several teams were already working on the development of private manned spacecraft. This first

X Prize provided additional incentive to spur the development of these vehicles, but it was not the only motivation. Commercial applications for space tourism and other purposes have long been envisaged.

Any group that musters the resources to fly a private rover to the Moon will need other motivations, however. The prize money will probably not cover the development costs of such a mission. One potential incentive could simply be kudos and adventure. Wealthy entrepreneurs have regularly sponsored expeditions on Earth aimed at exploration or discovery, and have often gone on these adventures themselves. With so many 'firsts' on Earth already achieved, sending a private mission to the Moon could be one of the few remaining ways for a rich person to gain a place in history.

But at least one team competing for the Google Lunar X Prize cites commercial applications for its mission. Technology developed for the lunar mission could be sold, or used to build commercial satellites. Another team is offering space for rent on its mission, allowing anything reasonable (such as scientific instruments or mementoes) to be carried. A US company called Celestis, which has been launching small vials of cremated human remains into space for years, has negotiated a deal with one team which will result in the transportation of human remains to the Moon for lunar burial. Another commercial deal involves landing a small telescope on the Moon as a test for a larger international lunar observatory.

For at least one team, winning the

prize alone would represent a commercial success. This team hopes to build a small lander and rover and launch them piggyback as a secondary payload on a commercial rocket launch. The total costs of the mission would be less than the value of the prize, if they succeed in this.

Landing by 2010?

Some teams have set themselves the goal of landing their rovers on the Moon by the end of 2010, which does not leave much time for these missions to fly. Can they do it? We will know very soon. Because the Google Lunar X Prize will gradually reduce in value if it is not won within a certain time frame, and will eventually become null, this provides an added incentive for teams to fly as quickly as possible.

If the prize is won, will other teams be deterred from continuing with their projects? For some, the prize is a secondary goal, and broader commercial interests will continue to drive the missions. Others will probably disappear quickly.

Private Manned Lunar Missions

Possibly the most ambitious concept that could be considered in private lunar exploration is a manned mission. Sending space tourists to the Moon on board a Russian Soyuz spacecraft (as mentioned in Chapter 15) would be a commercial flight, but would still use hardware operated by the Russian Government. Could a private company stage a lunar mission by itself?

One option suggests that this might be possible. SpaceX (Space Exploration Technologies), a US-based aerospace company, is developing a small fleet of cheap rockets for government and commercial launches. The first vehicle, Falcon 1, failed in three launch attempts before its fourth launch reached orbit successfully in September 2008. It is designed for launching small satellites into Earth orbit. Falcon 9, a larger vehicle, is designed to loft larger payloads. SpaceX has won funding from NASA to supply a cargo delivery service to the International Space Station, using a recoverable capsule known as Dragon. Dragon is a stubby, conical vehicle with a hatch in one side and a docking port at its front. A cylindrical service module at the rear of the capsule contains solar panels and other equipment to help Dragon fly in space. It looks a bit like an American Apollo spacecraft.

Early flights of Dragon in 2009 will carry equipment and no crew. But Dragon is expected to become a manned spacecraft, capable of flying as many as seven astronauts at once. It could be used to launch crews to the International Space Station, or on private space missions to commercial space habitats.

SpaceX is also working on a 'heavy' version of the Falcon 9 rocket. One SpaceX manager claims that this vehicle is capable of propelling Dragon on a circumlunar trajectory. It could fly to the Moon, loop around the far side, then return to Earth.

Will Dragon ever fly on such a mission? It's not clear if it will ever be sent on such a journey, or how it would be financed. SpaceX has announced no plans for such a mission, despite the

Dragon spacecraft with crew couches   SpaceX

Dragon spacecraft in cargo mode   SpaceX

Dragon spacecraft with docking hatch   SpaceX

technical feasibility. But it remains an option for the future.

Bigelow Aerospace

Bigelow Aerospace, a US aerospace firm, is developing inflatable space

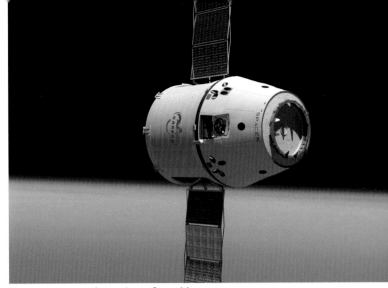

Dragon spacecraft in orbit   SpaceX

station modules. The skin of the modules is made from several layers of tough but flexible material. The modules are folded for launch, and inflate into larger structures when they are in orbit. Bigelow Aerospace has conducted two test launches with small-scale modules to prove the feasibility of the technology. These tests were successful, and have given the company the confidence to launch a larger module capable of supporting astronauts.

Bigelow Aerospace envisages the launch of a private space station, to be used by astronauts from various nations or to support private expeditions to space. A Bigelow Aerospace station could also be used for space tourism. Astronauts would be launched to the station on board Russian Soyuz spacecraft or other vehicles that may be available in the future.

Bigelow Aerospace is known to be considering the use of its inflatable modules for a lunar base. The modules would be softly landed on the surface of the Moon, then covered with lunar soil for protection against radiation. The timeframe anticipated in meeting this plan is unknown.

19 Science on the Moon

With the Moon already heavily probed by robot spacecraft and Apollo landings, how much science remains to be done there? A great deal, actually. The types of research that can be conducted on the Moon are very diverse, and are not limited to studying the Moon itself. This chapter provides an overview of some of the major themes that are being proposed for lunar science.

Astronomy

Astronomy from space has been practised for more than 30 years. The Hubble Space Telescope, which began operating in 1990, is one of the most famous objects ever launched into space. With no atmosphere around it, a telescope in space has a clear view. Similar conditions exist on the Moon. But why would anyone place a telescope on the Moon when they can already work in Earth orbit? The Moon offers a very stable anchor point in solid ground, allowing a telescope to be steered and pointed very precisely. The Moon is also positioned far beyond the Earth. It is not affected by the thin upper layers of the Earth's atmosphere, or by the magnetic and electrical fields that surround the Earth and can affect objects in Earth orbit.

In the near future, a robot lander could deploy a small telescope on the Moon, which would be operated by remote control. It would probably look similar to one on Earth. Some Moon telescopes would have covers to protect them when they are not in use.

Radio astronomy, using large dish antennas, is one of the most interesting segments of modern science but again, Earth's atmosphere and magnetic fields make it impossible to see certain frequencies. A radio telescope on the Moon would not have this problem.

Larger telescopes could be set up by astronauts to function automatically once they had left the Moon.

Astronauts deploy an array of optical telescopes   NASA

Looking Back at Earth

On Apollo 16, the astronauts deployed an astronomical camera to photograph the Earth from the Moon. This allowed

Apollo 16 landing site with rover   NASA

observations to be made of the Earth's upper atmosphere, from a perspective that not even an Earth satellite could match. The Kaguya spacecraft (2007) and other lunar orbiters have also observed the Earth from the vicinity of the Moon. The detail is not as great, but the entire planet can be observed simultaneously, in one observation.

Blocking out the Earth

An observatory on the far side of the Moon would never point at the Earth. Nothing on Earth itself would point directly at it, either. This would be highly useful for radio astronomy. Planet Earth is awash in radio signals, ranging from television broadcasts to mobile phones, which produce a lot of interference for instruments that are trying to pick up faint emissions from deep space. But the far side of the Moon is shadowed from these transmissions by the Moon itself. Signals can't pass through it.

Craters as Telescopes

The Arecibo radio telescope in Puerto Rico was built inside a natural crater formed by geological processes. The bowl shape of a crater is similar to the dish of a radio telescope. Scientists have proposed lining some lunar craters with reflective material, and using them as radio telescopes. It would not be possible to tilt the dishes, but they would gradually point in different directions as the Moon orbits the Earth.

Particle Physics

Some types of sub-atomic particles (such as cosmic rays) are blocked out by the Earth's magnetic field and atmosphere. This is beneficial, because many of them are harmful to life. But they are interesting to astronomers. Instruments on the Moon could detect these particles, just as they have been monitored by satellites. Some are emitted by the Sun, but most come from beyond the solar system.

Geology

Geology was the major type of scientific work undertaken by the Apollo astronauts, and it will continue to be practised on the Moon for decades. So many regions remain unexplored. The very structure of the Moon beneath its surface isn't well

Future lunar geology sampling will resemble Apollo procedures   NASA

Astronauts operate a drill attached to their rover   NASA

Astronauts erect instruments on the lunar surface   NASA

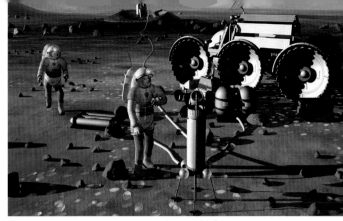

Astronauts operate a core sampler   NASA

well as other planets.

Lunar rocks are sometimes older than any rocks found on Earth. This is because the Moon has no weather patterns, liquid water or plate tectonics. To the frustration of geologists, the active nature of our own planet has destroyed much of its earliest composition, and lunar samples could provide some clues to what is missing. If fragments of these earliest rocks were dislodged by ancient meteorite impacts and deposited on the Moon, they could provide samples of our own world that simply cannot be found here.

Geology can be undertaken by robotic probes, but sending professional geologists to the Moon would be more productive. So far, the only professional geologist to visit the moon is Harrison Schmitt, who landed on Apollo 17, although every other Apollo astronaut was given geology training before his flight.

Rock samples will still be returned to Earth by future missions, but it will probably be more common for rocks to be examined where they are, or on board a nearby spacecraft. Hand-held instruments will allow some forms of testing to be performed without even picking a rock off the surface. These instruments could include lasers, which would blast away the outer layer of a

known. Understanding the geology of the Moon helps us to understand the formation and structure of the Earth, as

rock and allow geologists to study the composition of the vaporised sample.

Laboratory systems can be placed inside robot probes or inside spacecraft cabins. Future Moon landers will take microscopes, spectrometers and other instruments with them. The Apollo astronauts did not have the equipment, or the time, to undertake complex studies of the rocks they collected. In the 1960s, much of the apparatus used to examine rocks was too large to be transported to the Moon, but new technologies have changed this. A one-metre cube could contain an entire suite of small chemical laboratories, and be carried inside a spacecraft cabin. Rock and soil samples could be loaded into this device while the cabin was still exposed to the vacuum of space, then sealed. Automated tests could take place inside the device while the astronauts re-pressurised their spacecraft and removed their spacesuits.

Scientists on Earth could monitor the results of these experiments in real time across radio links. They could discuss the results with the astronauts (who would themselves have extensive training in geology) and propose new experiments or new objectives for the next Moon walk.

The samples returned to Earth would be carefully selected on the basis that particular information could only be obtained by bringing them back for more detailed analysis. It's probable that several dozen kilograms of rock could eventually be returned to Earth, but the total amount of material collected

and studied by the astronauts would be much larger.

Dust Migration and Electrical Charge
A newly emerging field of scientific inquiry on the Moon concerns dust migration. It was generally thought that Moon dust rarely moved, with impacts or electrostatic charges shifting it only slightly. Recent information from some robot probes, however, suggests that dust migrates more frequently and more extensively than previously suspected.

Measurable electrical charge differences can be produced between different locations on the Moon, such as the day and night side, due to the effects of charged particles from the Sun. The Moon also experiences electrostatic charging when it passes

Solar wind experiment on Apollo 11   NASA

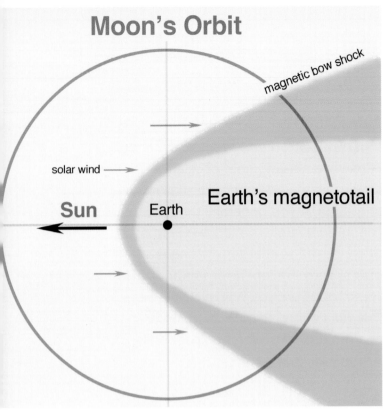

Magnetosphere of the Earth–Moon system   NASA/ Steele Hill

magnetically and electrically active, due to particles trapped in the magnetic field. The Moon passes through the magnetotail for a few days of each orbit of the Earth. During this time, dust migration could be more pronounced and there would also be stronger electrical and magnetic effects than at other times.

Dust migration will be investigated by robot spacecraft such as the proposed LADEE orbiter, and will be an ongoing area of study. Close investigations of dust movements and electrical phenomena will need to be undertaken.

through the Earth's magnetotail, an extension of the Earth's magnetic field that reaches deep into space. The magnetotail is 'stretched' by the influence of the solar wind, which is itself electrically charged. The boundary of this influence, where the solar wind pressures the Earth's magnetic field, is called 'bow shock'.

The stretched magnetotail produces a region in space that is both

Biology on the Moon

While the possibility of finding life on the Moon is extremely remote, and most astrobiologists pay scant attention to the subject, the Moon still has an important role to play in biological studies.

At some point, it would be useful to place a biosatellite in lunar orbit. This would be a spacecraft containing life forms that could range from bacteria to plant seeds to small animals.

Theory of dust movement caused by electrical charge   NASA/William Farrell

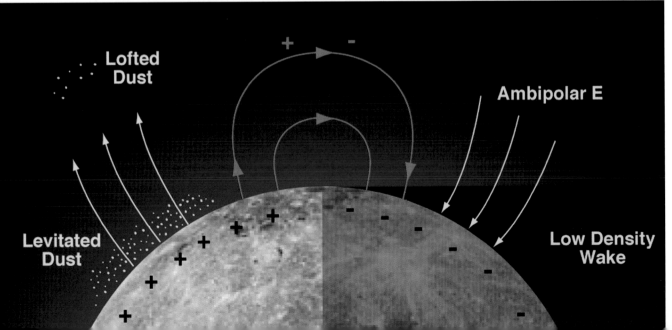

Foton class biosatellite   ESA

Biosatellites are regularly flown in Earth orbit, principally by Russia, with international participation. But the lunar orbit environment is potentially different from the Earth orbit environment. After spending a period of roughly two weeks in lunar orbit, the biosatellite would return to Earth. Scientists would examine the life forms on board for changes or ill-effects from their trip to the Moon.

A biological payload could also be landed on the Moon itself. This could be done by taking a box containing specimens on board a manned landing, or on an unmanned lunar lander. A biological experiment has been proposed for the European MoonNext lander. Designs for future robot sample-return missions could be modified to carry biological samples to the Moon and bring them back to Earth.

Exposing various types of biological tissue to lunar soil is one experiment that astronauts could perform during an extended stay on the surface. Other experiments could study the long-term effects of exposure to a low-gravity environment, which is poorly understood. Studies have been done already of the effects of microgravity (effectively, zero gravity or weightlessness) on astronauts and other living creatures. It's also possible to simulate some effects of low gravity by spinning small biological samples in a centrifuge on a space station, but this adds other forces that don't precisely duplicate the conditions of real low gravity. Going to the Moon is the only way to do this effectively.

20 Robot Wars

Since the space age began, a furious debate has raged through the scientific community. Is it worth sending humans into outer space?

Critics of human spaceflight cite numerous advantages for robot spaceflight. It's much cheaper, it's less complex, and it does not endanger human crews. They can point to the wonderful results that unmanned spacecraft have returned. All our planetary exploration has been carried out by robot spacecraft, and so has most of our lunar exploration.

So why should humans fly to the Moon, or anywhere else in space?

Some of the most common reasons put forward are emotional. We want to go. We want to explore. There is public appeal, and a sense of adventure.

Human spaceflight has always had a strong political overtone. It's not easy to achieve, and developing the capability to launch astronauts is rare on the international scene. Russia, the United States and China have all used their human spaceflight programs for political and propaganda purposes.

But there are also advantages of dexterity and judgment that no machine can hope to match. Human intervention has saved many space missions through repairs or the use of novel techniques, which can sometimes be as straightforward as unwinding a tangled cable. Robot space missions have routinely been compromised or lost when antennas or instrument covers failed to open. Fixing such problems are routine for a human astronaut.

The expertise and intelligence that can be supplied by a human expert can also be significant. In Earth orbit, human researchers act as laboratory technicians and scientists. On the Moon, their expertise in exploring the surface would be even more outstanding. The Apollo astronauts have already demonstrated this.

Critics of robot spaceflight have remarked that the Mars Exploration

European concept for a Moon base   ESA

Prototype Athlete rover for future US lunar exploration   NASA

rovers, which landed on that planet in 2004, take weeks to perform tasks that could be done in hours by human explorers. In the case of Mars, human spaceflight simply isn't an option at the present. But the opportunity exists on the Moon to use robots.

Robot explorers are getting more capable. Their sensors are more powerful, and their ability to act and navigate independently is steadily increasing. And although robots on the Moon will probably surpass the capabilities of the very robust rovers sent to Mars, they will still be no match for a well-trained human.

Of course, behind every robot mission lies a team of expert humans who control the spacecraft. Human explorers on the Moon will also be heavily dependent on machines, and the instruments they bring with them. The real future of lunar exploration will be a fusion of human and robotic capabilities, with each being used to its best advantages. Robots are more suited to global mapping and spot-checks on certain locations, while human explorers can perform complex tasks and investigations.

Astronaut inspects a robotic rover   NASA

Spaceflight advocates also point out that space is more than just exploration and adventure. They foresee a time when large numbers of people could live in space. Our spaceflight activities are preparing us for the time when space will be opened for all of us.

Athlete rovers with lunar base modules   NASA

21 Survival on the Moon

Spaceflight of any form poses risks and dangers. But flying to the Moon, and staying on the Moon, presents unique challenges. Most human spaceflight is in Earth orbit, which gives astronauts a relatively strong level of protection from the hazards encountered in deep space. The long-term effects of keeping humans in a near-Earth space environment are fairly well understood, and flights of several months on space stations are carried out routinely. By contrast, the lunar environment and its effects on humans have barely been examined.

Deep Space and Radiation

Anything beyond Earth orbit is generally known as 'deep space'. Voyages to the Moon fall within this category. A spacecraft in deep space is exposed to particles, magnetic fields and radiation conditions that are vastly different from low Earth orbit. The spacecraft has moved away from the protection of the Earth's magnetic field, which provides shielding against some forms of radiation to Earth orbital missions.

Studies of the radiation environment in the space around the Moon have mostly been aimed at understanding solar physics and the properties of interplanetary space. They have not generally focused on assessing the health risks to astronauts.

Instruments on new missions such as the Lunar Reconnaissance Orbiter are attempting to address these questions. This spacecraft is carrying samples of plastic that simulate the radiation absorption of human tissue. Plastic material like this is commonly used to calibrate medical equipment on Earth.

Tissue equivalent plastic, used in radiation experiments
Standard Imaging

Radiation experiment for Lunar Reconnaissance Orbiter   Harlan Spence/Boston University

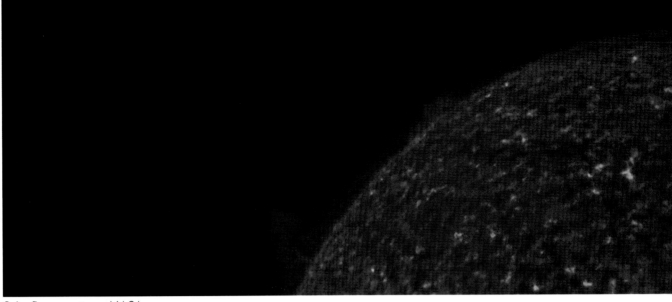

Solar flare eruption   NASA

Radiation levels are measured with the aid of a small, wedged-shaped instrument package on the exterior of the spacecraft. The Chandrayaan-1 orbiter from India also carries a radiation-measuring instrument.

Similar experiments performed on board a Mars orbiter suggest that deep space has a significantly higher level of radiation than near-Earth space. It remains to be seen if space in lunar orbit will pose the same risks as Mars.

Exposure to higher levels of radiation could be tolerable for short missions to the Moon. But astronauts staying there for extended periods could experience health problems if countermeasures are not taken. Doctors are concerned that extended missions could increase the risks of cancer.

Of all the hazards of lunar exploration, radiation is arguably the most serious. It is also one of the most difficult to counteract. New medicines could be introduced to counteract the cellular damage produced by radiation, but it remains to be seen if this would be effective. Radiation shielding for spacecraft and lunar bases will be essential.

Solar Flares

A particularly nasty form of radiation in deep space comes from solar flares, the huge bursts of particles and energy that are regularly released from the Sun, shooting into space. Sometimes these flares cause problems with satellites in Earth orbit, or even disrupt power generation on Earth. Solar flares cause massive increases in radiation levels in deep space, especially in the inner solar system. They could be lethal to astronauts on the Moon if they did not have shielding against radiation. Solar flare-bursts are now routinely monitored by satellites that watch the Sun, and bulletins are regularly circulated. Warnings of an emerging solar flare could be transmitted quickly to astronauts on the Moon, prompting them to retreat to their spacecraft, or even to enter a special shielded chamber inside the spacecraft.

Biohazards and Infection

Samples of lunar soil returned by Apollo missions were extensively studied for their effects on biological specimens. The first Apollo crews to return from the Moon were quarantined

Apollo astronauts in quarantine suits   NASA

upon their return in case they were infected with harmful pathogens. They were required to wear biological isolation garments when they emerged from their spacecraft, suits which totally enclose the body and filter all air passing in and out. The astronauts were later housed in an isolation facility. For the crew of Apollo 11, quarantine lasted two weeks.

Today, it is generally agreed that the Moon does not present any indigenous biohazards to astronauts who go there, or to planet Earth when they return. Quarantine of rocks and astronauts for the purpose of containing biohazards is unlikely to occur on future missions.

But infection can still be a problem in the enclosed environment of a spacecraft or lunar base, if pathogens are brought along from Earth. Astronauts could have their immune systems weakened by exposure to weightlessness or the reduced gravity of the Moon. Quarantining astronauts for some weeks before lift-off, and subjecting them to thorough medical examinations before flight, should reduce this risk.

(Right) Apollo surface operations   NASA

Particle Inhalation

Dust and particle inhalation pose a serious health risk on Earth—respiratory diseases are commonly caused by such particles. As yet there has been little study of the potential hazards to astronauts of exposure to lunar dust. On the Apollo missions, dust was widely circulated and even inhaled. The astronauts found that it smelled like gunpowder. Controlling lunar dust will be tricky. It is often charged with static electricity, tends to cling to anything it touches—and it is inescapable. Preventing dust inhalation could become an issue for long-term lunar missions.

Partial Gravity

The lunar gravity is roughly one sixth that of Earth. This makes many tasks easier to perform than in the weightlessness of orbital spaceflight, where objects float around. Partial gravity can make locomotion difficult on the lunar surface, however, especially when astronauts are wearing cumbersome spacesuits. The Apollo astronauts sometimes fell over.

Partial gravity could pose problems for the astronauts who stay on the Moon for a long period. The influence of low gravity is barely understood. The effects of weightlessness on the human body have been studied extensively with space station crews, but our only experience with partial gravity has come from the Apollo missions. Only twelve astronauts have experienced these conditions, and only for relatively short periods. There is no evidence that partial gravity caused them any health problems, but over long periods it could have effects. Some of these could be similar to, if less severe than, the effects of weightlessness. Muscles could grow weaker, bones could lose calcium and overall fitness could change.

To offset the effects of partial gravity on the body, it is anticipated that regular exercise will be a part of the routine of any crew of a lunar base.

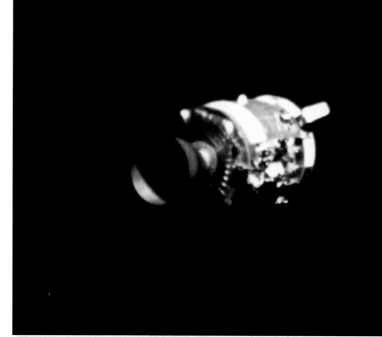

The damaged service module from Apollo 13   NASA

Equipment Failure
Missions in Earth orbit have the option of returning to Earth quickly in the event of equipment failure. But for a mission flying to the Moon, or on the Moon, return to Earth takes longer. The flight of Apollo 13, which experienced an explosion in an oxygen tank en route to the Moon, demonstrated the hazards of equipment failure in deep space. It took several days to nudge the crippled spacecraft back to Earth.

Landed missions will presumably have an 'emergency return' option, allowing crewmembers to enter their vehicle and quickly take off. A mission staying for an extended period would need redundancy (backup) in their essential equipment, allowing spare components to be quickly switched on if a main component failed.

Creating a space station in lunar orbit could offer a safe haven for endangered crews on the lunar surface, giving them access to life support without the long journey back to Earth.

Moonquakes
Scientists are becoming concerned that some parts of the Moon are simply unsafe for landing. Seismic activity, caused by gas venting from beneath the surface, could cause the ground to either shake or collapse, destroying anything nearby. The exact risk posed by this type of activity has not been precisely determined, but some of the upcoming robot missions will help to reveal the real nature of this potential risk.

Meteoroid Impacts
A lunar lander, staying on the Moon for only a short time, has a minimal chance of being hit by a meteoroid. But a

larger base, with an operational lifetime of a decade or more, could encounter several small micrometeoroid impacts. Protection against these impacts would be necessary. Metal layers, or lunar soil shovelled over the base, would be suitable.

The chance of a very large impact is small, but still possible. At the moment, the exact threat posed by meteoroid impacts on the Moon is poorly understood. Further research will need to be done before large bases are constructed.

22   Helium-3: Energy from the Moon?

Discussions of lunar missions in the twenty-first century have often featured the tantalising prospect that the Moon could offer a source of clean, abundant energy for the world. Some groups think that mining the Moon could help our energy-hungry planet solve many of the economic, political and environmental problems that dominate our headlines. But is this realistic?

Fusion Power

Nuclear reactors have supplied energy to the world for decades. They operate on the principle of nuclear fission, where the atoms of heavy elements (such as uranium and plutonium) are broken down into smaller atoms, releasing energy in the process. But another type of energy-generating nuclear reaction, known as fusion, is possible. Nuclear fusion occurs when the atoms of very light elements (such as hydrogen or helium) are 'fused', or squeezed together, to form heavier atoms. Fusion is the mechanism that powers the Sun and other stars. In some ways, Earth has used fusion energy throughout its entire history.

Nuclear fusion only occurs under extreme conditions of heat and pressure, such as in the centre of stars. Fusion reactions have also been generated on Earth. Thermonuclear

weapons (hydrogen bombs) generate most of their explosive force through fusion. Small, contained fusion reactions are also generated regularly in laboratories.

So far, nobody has built a reliable, practical fusion reactor. Fusion reactors

Interior of Joint European Torus, an experimental fusion reactor   EFDA-JET

(Below) Exterior of Joint European Torus   EFDA-JET

Schematic diagram of Joint European Torus   EFDA-JET

A technician inspects the interior of the Joint European Torus   EFDA-JET

are a long way from being as reliable as the fission reactors used to power cities, but research aimed at developing fusion power reactors is being aggressively pursued at laboratories around the world. Most designs for fusion reactors feature large, donut-shaped chambers surrounded by magnets. Magnetic fields are used to contain a super-hot ring of electrified gas called a 'plasma' inside the reactor, which undergoes fusion. Billions of dollars are being invested in fusion research by multinational groups. Despite this, nobody knows when, or if, we will eventually see fusion power become a reality.

Helium-3

Samples of Moon rocks returned by the Apollo astronauts held a surprise. The Moon's surface holds considerable quantities of helium-3, a rare form of helium gas. Helium-3 is lighter than normal helium, due to the absence of a sub-atomic particle inside its atoms. The helium-3 is believed to have been deposited on the Moon by the solar wind, which has washed over the unprotected lunar surface for aeons.

A fusion reactor could be operated with regular helium or even hydrogen, depending on its design. But helium-3 is regarded as premium fuel for fusion reactors. It offers the prospect of yielding high energy with little radioactivity or pollution.

Visionaries and engineers have long wondered at the possibility of mining helium-3 on the Moon and transporting it back to Earth. The idea has been around for a long time, but discussion of this concept has escalated in recent years.

Politics and Energy

The twenty-first century has been gripped by concerns over energy. Demand for energy-generating minerals is escalating around the world, especially as the populous nations of China and India undergo strong economic growth. Geopolitical tensions are rising as nations try to secure access to oil, natural gas, coal and uranium.

In such troubled times, the prospect of a new source of energy is particularly tantalising. Wishful thinking may prompt some groups to overlook the uncertainties of helium-3 energy, and allow themselves to believe that it will rescue us from our current problems.

China has occasionally mentioned the significance of helium-3 on the Moon as a motivating factor in its own lunar exploration. Locating helium-3 deposits has been stated as one of several scientific goals of the Chang'e-1 orbiter mission.

But it is unclear if China is strongly committed to the idea of mining the Moon. Managers within the space program could be trumpeting the concept to their political masters as a way of gaining financial support for spaceflight, even if they quietly hold doubts about their own pronouncements. Official media statements about the potential of helium-3 could also be seen as a way of justifying space exploration to the general public. Exactly what is believed by different organs within the Chinese government is difficult to fathom.

Some scientists may genuinely believe that helium-3 from the Moon will solve the energy problems of China and other nations, but others may simply be using the claim to gain support for their ventures.

It's easy to make such claims when there is no firm evidence to disprove them, and real fusion power remains years away. By the time the matter is conclusively resolved—and that could be several decades into the future— many of the people now advocating helium-3 mining will have retired, and other technologies could have superseded the need for it.

Science or Fiction?

Any speculation about mining the Moon for helium-3 needs to be somewhat measured. It must be remembered that we do not currently have anything close to an operational prototype of a fusion power reactor. It is not clear if any such prototype would require helium-3 to operate, or even if it would be compatible with the reactor's design. If helium-3 proves to be desirable, it could also be extracted from the oceans or helium gas pockets on Earth. The complexities of mining this substance on the Moon, then transporting it to Earth, could be prohibitive.

In the event that helium-3 mining proves viable, how would it be done? Some plans envisage robot collectors driving across the surface, scooping up the soil beneath them and baking out the helium, then jettisoning the spent soil behind them. The collected

Helium for fusion reactors could be easier to mine on Earth   NASA

helium-3 would need to be liquefied for transport. An advanced form of spacecraft would be needed to transport it safely to Earth. So far, nobody has demonstrated any detailed plans or equipment for carrying out these tasks.

The Near Term

The next decade should provide some fairly solid advances in the state of fusion power research. A large new research reactor is being constructed in France. It is possible that fusion power generation could be demonstrated within 20 years, by which time spaceflight technology should also have advanced. Once a prototype fusion reactor is constructed, the path from there to mass use of fusion power will also be lengthy, and will probably take another decade.

The first fusion power reactors will almost certainly not be powered by helium-3 from the Moon, however, but by the more common helium-4, which makes up most of the helium gas found on Earth.

This outline is speculative, but fusion research has always been subject to delays and disappointments. Nobody really knows when, or if, practical fusion power will become a reality.

23 Life on the Moon

Space explorers are currently obsessed with finding life in space. There could be life buried deep underground on Mars, or beneath the frozen ice surfaces of the moons of Jupiter and Saturn. This would be simple life, no larger than single-celled bacteria. But the discovery of life beyond our own planet would be the greatest scientific breakthrough of the twenty-first century. Might anything be found on the Moon?

Barren Rocks

Modern science has always taken a dim view of the prospect of life on the Moon. It lacks an atmosphere and suffers from extreme temperature variations. Photographs show rocks and soil, but nothing alive.

Lunar soil samples retrieved by astronauts were searched for life forms or fossils. Nothing was found. Scientists tried growing bacteria in water that had been mixed with lunar soil, and found that some bacterial growth was harmed by the chemicals in the soil. The lack of water in most regions of the Moon is also a problem.

However, experiments that involved growing plants in lunar soil returned to Earth were more successful, which suggests that lunar minerals are not hazardous to all life.

No Quarantine

The first three crews to land on the Moon were placed in quarantine when they returned to Earth. This was to ensure that they had not been infected by any viruses or bacteria from the Moon. Most doctors thought that this was not really necessary, but NASA did not want to take chances with public safety.

It was quickly discovered that the astronauts carried no infections, and the samples returned from the Moon contained no life at all. So quarantine was not required for the crews that followed. It is unlikely to be used on any future astronauts returning from the Moon.

Life at the Poles?

The presence of water-ice in shadowed craters at the polar regions, where the lunar surface is protected from extreme temperatures, has been confirmed. Water is an essential ingredient for life. Could there be microorganisms in these areas?

Some scientists have suggested that bacteria and other microorganisms could travel around in space inside comets and meteors, which thus could have delivered living organisms to Earth, Mars and elsewhere. Comets regularly strike the Moon, and some have deposited the water found at the

Hypervelocity gas gun at the University of Kent is used to simulate meteorite impacts   M. Burchell/University of Kent

Kent have conducted experiments with 'hypervelocity impacts', simulating the way comets and meteors hit the Moon and planets. Gas guns are used to fire pellets at targets, and the impacts are monitored. Burchell believes that it could be possible for bacteria to survive an impact with the Moon.

But—getting life to survive after arrival is another matter. Chemicals in the rocks and soil that any such bacteria encountered on the Moon could destroy them. Radiation could also be hazardous. There could also be a lack of an energy source, such as light or food, for metabolism. In theory, some life could survive by going dormant for an extended period in the extreme cold. Bacteria on Earth have been discovered, frozen in ice, with an estimated age of roughly 120,000 years. This is a long period of time, but it is not clear if the bacteria could survive for much longer intervals. The level of background radiation on the Moon could also steadily degrade the genetic material of bacteria over a long period, even if they were relatively well protected by rocks and other material.

Scientists working in astrobiology generally feel that life on the Moon is not totally impossible, but most unlikely.

poles. Could they have brought life to the Moon?

It would be difficult.

In the first instance, nobody is really sure that life hitchhikes on comets and meteors. This is a controversial theory that is not universally accepted.

In the second place, the Moon has no atmosphere to slow down an incoming object. Objects hitting the Moon strike at tremendous speed. However, Professor Mark Burchell and a team of scientists at the University of

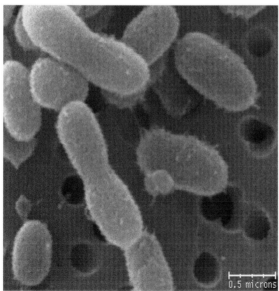

0.5 microns

120,000 year-old bacteria from Earth   Jennifer Loveland-Curtze, Penn State University

Bacterial Survival?

The Apollo 12 mission landed near a robot Surveyor spacecraft that had touched down several years earlier. Parts of the robot craft were removed by the astronauts and returned to Earth, to see how they had weathered from exposure to space. The scientists who examined them were surprised to discover Streptococcus bacteria. This was not thought to be evidence of indigenous life on the Moon, however, but of organisms that had stowed away before launch, and survived for years on the lunar surface.

Nobody knows whether bacteria did survive, or could survive, several years on the Moon. It is possible that the bacteria were introduced to the Surveyor parts after they were returned to Earth. It is also possible that the bacteria really did make a round trip to the Moon and back, and were protected by the spacecraft's components from the extreme conditions on the Moon.

Discussion of the Surveyor bacterial incident, once controversial, is no longer active within the scientific community. It was not part of a rigorously controlled experiment and is considered inconclusive.

Material from Earth

Scientists think it is possible that millions of years ago rocks could have been blown off the newly-forming planet Earth by meteorite impacts and floated through space to the Moon. Given the proliferation of life on Earth, it is possible that life could have been transported to the Moon in this way. But could it have survived? It seems unlikely, in light of the aforementioned conditions. It could be envisaged that a rock from Earth, laden with bacteria, could land in a water-rich region at the poles, spreading life in a little frozen pool. But the probability of this occurring seems very low.

Surveyor 3 is inspected by Apollo 12 astronauts   NASA

Lunar Ecosystem

The European Space Agency is considering the launch of the first astrobiology experiment to be conducted on the Moon. This would involve a small collection of microorganisms from Earth, to be carried aboard the MoonNext lander. One group of microorganisms would consume oxygen and produce carbon dioxide, the other would consume carbon dioxide and produce oxygen. The experiment would act like a small ecosystem, with the different organisms feeding each other. Sunlight reaching the lunar surface would be the energy source. The survival of the organisms under lunar conditions would be monitored remotely.

Eventually, larger ecosystems could be created on the Moon, and lunar bases could use green plants for generating food and oxygen, as well as recycling waste products. The first lunar bases, however, are unlikely to depend on biological systems for life support.

STOP PRESS: Indian Space Capsule Options

As this book went to press, information on India's plans for launching its own astronauts aboard its own space launch vehicle began to emerge. Some of this information was incorporated into chapter 11. This 'stop press' segment supplies additional information on this important development.

India has announced plans for the construction of an astronaut training centre on its own soil. It has also decided to recruit astronaut trainees from among the ranks of the country's space scientists and engineers. This is an interesting departure from practices in Russia, the United States and China, which all exclusively recruited military pilots for their first batches of astronauts and cosmonauts. Personnel from ISRO, the Indian Space Research Organisation, are expected to become astronaut candidates.

The design of India's manned space capsule had not been announced at the time of writing, and it is possible that much of the basic design was still unresolved, although it was revealed that it would draw heavily upon the design of the Russian Soyuz spacecraft, which had previously influenced the design of China's Shenzhou spacecraft.

This announcement was made in late 2008, with launch of the spacecraft planned for 2015. This is a relatively short development and test window for a new spacecraft, thus it could be expected that India would try to use as much existing infrastructure and technology as possible.

India has the option of adapting technology from the Space Recovery Experiment, which flew a small re-entry capsule successfully in 2007. The SRE capsule was a blunt cone which stayed in orbit for twelve days, performing microgravity experiments. It re-entered nose first, with its surface covered by protective heatshield tiles, and was recovered after parachuting to an ocean splashdown.

The illustrations in this segment are unofficial artist's impressions, depicting

Three possible variations for an Indian spacecraft   Morris Jones

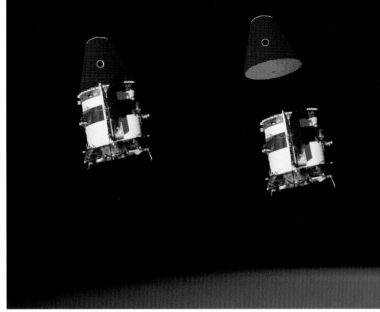

Re-entry separation sequence for Indian manned spacecraft   Morris Jones

a possible set of configurations for the Indian manned spacecraft. This assumes that the crew will ride in an SRE-inspired re-entry capsule, with a service module at its rear assumed to be similar to the one used on Soyuz. It is possible that these two modules will be enough for the first spacecraft, although a third 'orbital module' could be placed in front of the re-entry capsule to supply extra room for the crew. This could resemble the ovoid shape used on Soyuz, or the cylindrical one used on the Chinese Shenzhou spacecraft. The spacecraft would need a large set of solar panels (which have not been included in the illustration).

At the end of the mission, rocket engines in the service module would fire to pull the spacecraft out of orbit, and the re-entry module would separate from the service module. Two astronauts are expected to fly for roughly one week on the first mission.

Another option would be to elect to use the same overall design as Soyuz, with contemporary modifications to the vehicle's instrumentation and computer systems. The resemblance would be very strong.

More than one test mission would need to be flown before the new spacecraft could be considered safe for astronauts. This suggests the need to launch a prototype by 2013 or 2014, further shortening the development time.

India's Geosynchronous Satellite Launch Vehicle (GSLV) will need to be modified to accommodate the spacecraft. This will involve the addition of a launch escape system, probably resembling the small escape rocket found at the top of Soyuz and Shenzhou launch vehicles. The escape rocket pulls the spacecraft free of the main rocket in the event of a launch problem. The GSLV will probably need vibration dampeners to protect the crew, and other modifications as well.

The announcement of the Soyuz connection was a surprise to some observers. Earlier provisional artwork had suggested that the Indian spacecraft would be a large cone, similar in shape to the SRE capsule, with a small instrument and retrorocket package at its rear, and two solar panels. This indicates that a change in program structure has taken place, possibly in reaction to the large costs and long development schedules that would be experienced with a totally home-grown program.

The Indian manned space program is an ambitious feat with an ambitious time schedule. Nonetheless, given the country's technology base, it should be feasible to meet these goals.

Bibliography

Information on these issues changes so rapidly that online sources remain the best way to keep pace with events. The following websites are recommended:

The British Interplanetary Society
  JBIS (Journal of the British Interplanetary Society)
  Space Chronicle
  Spaceflight magazine
  www.bis-spaceflight.com

China Lunar Exploration Program (CLEP)
http://210.82.31.82

China Manned Space Engineering (CMSE)
www.cmse.gov.cn

China National Space Administration
www.cnsa.gov.cn

European Space Agency
www.esa.int

Indian Space Research Organisation (ISRO)
www.isro.gov.in

Japan Space Exploration Agency (JAXA)
www.jaxa.jp

Jet Propulsion Laboratory
www.jpl.nasa.gov

Korea Aerospace Research Institute (KARI)
www.kari.re.kr

Moon Daily
www.moondaily.com

NASA
www.nasa.gov

Space Daily
www.spacedaily.com

Acknowledgments

The author appreciates the assistance of the following institutions and individuals:

Aero News Network
Analytical Graphics, Inc.
Armadillo Aerospace
Boston University
Chinese Consulate, Sydney
Philippe Coue
Kerrie Dougherty
EADS-Astrium
EFDA-Joint European Torus
Doug Ellison
European Space Agency
Indian Space Research Organisation (ISRO)
Japan Space Exploration Agency (JAXA)
Jet Propulsion Laboratory
KAIST (Korea)
Korean Aerospace Research Institute

Chen Lan
Lockheed Martin
Los Alamos National Laboratory
NASA
Naval Research Laboratory (USA)
Northrop Grumman
Penn State University
Powerhouse Museum, Sydney
Rutherford Appelton Laboratory
Malcolm Smith
SpaceX. Space Adventures
Standard Imaging
Starsem
STFC (UK)
Surrey Satellite Technology Limited
Thejes (India)
University of Arizona
University of California Los Angeles
University of Kent
Charles Vick
X Prize Foundation

Index